Faith

MODERN WORLD

Timeless Biblical Principles for Overcoming Contemporary Challenges

Oluwagbemiga Oyeneye

TRILOGY
PROFESSIONAL PUBLISHING MEETS POWERFUL PROMOTION

A wholly owned subsidiary of TBN

Trilogy Christian Publishers
A Wholly Owned Subsidiary of Trinity Broadcasting Network
2442 Michelle Drive
Tustin, CA 92780
Copyright © 2024 by Oluwagbemiga Oyeneye
Scripture quotations marked AMPC are taken from the Amplified® Bible, Classic Edition (AMPC), Copyright © 2015 by The Lockman Foundation. Used by permission. www.Lockman.org.
Scripture quotations marked CEV are taken from the Contemporary English Version®. Copyright © 1995 American Bible Society. All rights reserved.
Scripture quotations marked ESV are taken from the ESV® Bible (The Holy Bible, English Standard Version®), copyright © 2001 by Crossway Bibles, a publishing ministry of Good News Publishers. Used by permission. All rights reserved.
Scripture quotations marked NIV are taken from THE HOLY BIBLE, NEW INTERNATIONAL VERSION®, NIV® Copyright © 1973, 1978, 1984, 2011 by Biblica, Inc.® Used by permission. All rights reserved worldwide.

Scripture quotations marked NKJV are taken from the New King James Version®. Copyright © 1982 by Thomas Nelson. Used by permission. All rights reserved. Scripture quotations marked NLT are taken from the Holy Bible, New Living Translation, copyright © 1996, 2004, 2015 by Tyndale House Foundation. Used by permission of Tyndale House Publishers, Inc., Carol Stream, Illinois 60188. All rights reserved.
All rights reserved, including the right to reproduce this book or portions there in any form whatsoever.
For information, address Trilogy Christian Publishing
Rights Department, 2442 Michelle Drive, Tustin, CA 92780.
Trilogy Christian Publishing/ TBN and colophon are trademarks of Trinity Broadcasting Network.
For information about special discounts for bulk purchases, please contact Trilogy Christian Publishing. Trilogy Disclaimer: The views and content expresse in this book are those of the author and may not necessarily reflect the views and doctrine of Trilogy Christian Publishing or the Trinity Broadcasting Network.

10 9 8 7 6 5 4 3 2 1
Library of Congress Cataloging-in-Publication Data is available.
ISBN 979-9-89041-760-2 | ISBN (ebook) 979-9-89041-761-9

TABLE OF CONTENTS

Dedication 3

Introduction I Might Not Encounter Goliath 5

Chapter 1: Seizing Opportunities: Why Preparation is Key to Success 13

Chapter 2: Building Your Boats 30

Chapter 3: Breaking Through Limitations: Overcoming Systems and Structures 58

Chapter 4: The Return of a Son 82

Chapter 5: And He Went Out, Not Knowing Where He Was Going 108

Chapter 6: Frame Your World 131

Chapter 7: Obtain Your Good Report 150

Acknowledgement 161

Stay Connected 164

DEDICATION

For my wife, Adijat Bola Oyeneye,

Thank you for being by my side on this journey of faith.

INTRODUCTION

I Might Not Encounter Goliath

A line from one of my favorite songs resonates deeply: I might not encounter Goliath, but I certainly have my own significant battles—my own giants. In this journey called life, these words echo the profound truth that our struggles, though unique from those faced in Biblical times, are no less formidable. They are the mountains we must climb, the battles we must conquer. The line from this song is about the story of David, a young shepherd boy of about seventeen years, who volunteers to fight a Philistine giant, Goliath. Goliath is said to have been over nine feet tall, heavily armored, and vastly experienced in all forms of war. As the champion of the Philistines, Goliath challenges the Israelites to send out their champion to fight him in single combat, with the winner deciding the outcome of the entire battle. The Israelites were intimidated by Goliath and unwilling to step up to fight against him. That's when David arrives on the scene and volunteers to fight Goliath. In a dramatic fashion that would undoubtedly capture any reader of this story, David triumphed over Goliath, showing how faith in God can guarantee victory even when faced with difficult odds.

The modern-day believer is familiar with stories like this one and numerous others in the Bible, where people faced insurmountable odds, overcame challenges, defeated their enemies, and entered the promises of God for their lives. Therefore, "have faith in God" is almost the standard biblical response when facing challenges. Jesus gave the same answer to His disciples after what could be described as the "fig tree miracle." Jesus entered a town with His disciples and saw a fig tree He hoped to eat from. But when He got close to the tree, He found only leaves, not fruit. Then He said, "Let no one eat fruit from you ever again." The next day, the disciples saw that the fig tree had dried up, just as Jesus said it would. In response to the surprise of His disciples, Jesus said, "Have faith in God." In other words, faith accomplished what seemed impossible to the natural man. Someone said you can end many conversations with just that statement, "Have faith in God."

However, the Bible was written over thousands of years, with the earliest parts of the Old Testament dating back to around 1500 BCE. In those times, people lived in a much more primitive and agrarian society with no modern technology or conveniences. They relied on subsistence farming and animal husbandry to survive, and their lives were often complex and fraught with danger.

Over time, however, human societies evolved and developed new technologies and ways of living. The Industrial Revolution of the 18th and 19th centuries marked a significant turning point as machines began to take over many of the tasks previously done by hand. The Industrial Revolution led to the rise of urbanization and the growth of cities as people moved from rural areas to work in factories and other industrial settings.

Today, we live in an age of rapid technological change, with computers, smartphones, and the internet transforming almost every aspect of our lives. New social issues and cultural trends are emerging at a rapid pace. We have access to information and entertainment on a scale that would have been unimaginable just a few decades ago, and we can communicate with people worldwide in real time.

While these changes bring new opportunities and experiences, they can create confusion, anxiety, and uncertainty. Moreover, what the future will hold as we continue to navigate this rapidly changing world remains to be seen. As times change, the challenges and contexts we face also change. Amid these challenges, many people turn to faith as a source of strength and guidance.

Perhaps, like most people, you realize the need to have faith in God to move your mountains. From early childhood, you have memorized stories from the Bible that demonstrate faith in God. You know what David did when he faced Goliath; you know in grand detail how Daniel's faith helped him survive the lion's Den; you know what Hannah did when she was waiting to have her child. All these stories have provided various practices of what faith accomplished in other people's lives. Hebrews Chapter 11 is described as the faith chapter. In this chapter, we see numerous examples of what was achieved through the faith of biblical heroes. Almost every verse begins with "by faith" and then the feat that was accomplished. In this chapter, you'd see that by faith, they obtained righteousness, got divine warnings, received strength for conception, subdued kingdoms, stopped the mouths of lions, quenched the violence of fire, escaped the sword's edge, and many more testimonies.

Nevertheless, it is very doubtful that you would face off against a nine-foot giant in winner-takes-all single combat as David did or get thrown into a lion's den like Daniel. The challenges you face today are different from those encountered in biblical times, but that doesn't make them any less significant or impactful. You may not be fighting physical battles against towering giants like Goliath today.

Still, you face daily giants in societal, economic, and personal challenges.

****

> "For whatever things were written before were written for our learning, that we through the patience and comfort of the Scriptures might have hope."
>
> **Romans 15:4 NKJV**

Despite the challenges of modern-day living, the Bible provides us with timeless principles of faith. As we see in Romans 15:4, the stories, and examples we find in the scriptures are for our learning. We are to draw wisdom and faith applications from these stories to our situations. Nonetheless, most people find applying these principles to their modern lives challenging. The cultural and contextual backgrounds of the biblical stories are vastly different from the world we live in today, making it hard to draw practical applications from them. Essentially, knowing how to apply biblical principles to the complex issues we face in our daily lives can be difficult.

Today's common challenge is bridging the gap between principles of faith found in the Bible and their application to modern-day challenges. While the Bible provides timeless truths and principles that apply to all aspects of life, understanding how to use these principles in contemporary situations can be challenging.

However, the power of the Bible lies in its ability to transcend time and culture, and you can still apply its principles of faith to your life today. It is important to remember that *the challenges we face may be different. Still, the underlying tenets of faith remain the same.* We can learn from the examples of faith displayed in the Bible and apply those same principles to our own lives.

Therefore, this book aims to explore how biblical principles of faith can provide practical solutions to some of the most pressing contemporary challenges we face. The book will help to bridge the gap between principles of faith found in the Bible and their application to modern-day challenges. We will examine topics such as:

Preparing for an unknown future.

Breaking barriers to growth.

Following God's leading.

Walking in perfect understanding of your righteous standing with God.

Framing your world through your words.

I will draw on examples from the Bible to provide insights and guidance on navigating contemporary Christian issues. I will show how faith can provide a foundation for living a more fulfilling and purposeful life through biblical teaching and real-world examples.

Whether you are a long-time believer looking to deepen your faith or someone exploring spirituality for the first time, this book will provide tools and inspiration for overcoming contemporary challenges and living a life of greater purpose and meaning. By recognizing the differences in cultural and contextual backgrounds between the Bible and our modern world, we can better understand the principles of faith and how to apply them in our daily lives. So, join me on this journey of faith and discover how you can use timeless wisdom contained in the Bible to face the challenges of the modern world.

To do this, I explored modern challenges people face and matched them with their biblical equivalent. Then, I drew on the faith principles contained in the Bible's examples to apply them to our modern-day challenges.

This book is divided into chapters. At the end of the chapters, I suggested some prayers and confessions to get you started in your walk of faith. Also, you will find reflective questions that I will encourage you to explore more deeply. I've provided you with an opportunity to write down your reflections and actions items after reading each chapter, through the dedicated "Action Note" section. I hope you find the journey of faith inspiring as I have and that this book stirs up your faith in many more ways than you ever imagined.

CHAPTER 1

Seizing Opportunities: Why Preparation is Key to Success

> "It is better to be prepared for an opportunity and not have one than to have an opportunity and not be prepared."
>
> **- Whitney M. Young, Jr., American Civil Rights Leader.**

In 2011, Evan Spiegel, Bobby Murphy, and Reggie Brown, students at Stanford University, developed an app called Picaboo. They designed the app as a way for users to send disappearing photos and videos to each other. Spiegel and his team had been trying to get funding for their app for months but could not secure any investors. However, Spiegel had the opportunity to pitch his app during a meeting with a venture capitalist named Jeremy Liew.

Liew was impressed by the app's potential and offered to invest in the company on the spot. However, Spiegel was not prepared to accept the investment. He had no idea how to structure a deal, the terms, or how much equity to give up. As a result, Liew withdrew his offer, and the company was left without funding. Spiegel later admitted that he was unprepared for the opportunity and had let his lack of experience hold him back. However, he learned from his mistake and eventually secured funding for his app from other investors.

In 2012, the app was renamed Snapchat, and it quickly gained popularity among young people to share funny or silly moments with friends without leaving a permanent digital record. The app's unique feature of disappearing messages and stories became a hit. Snapchat rapidly grew in popularity, especially among the younger demographic. Today, Snapchat's popularity has made it a significant player in the social media landscape. It is currently a multi-billion-dollar company with millions of users worldwide.

The initial setback faced by Spiegel, which left the founders without funding, is something that most people can relate to today. Many people find themselves at the right place and time. Still, they are not prepared to take advantage of the opportunities that come their way. In this lesson of adequately preparing for opportunities, Jesus shared an instructive example in Matthew 25: 1-13. The fictitious story Jesus tells is about ten virgins waiting for a bridegroom to arrive so they can attend a wedding banquet. Five of the virgins are wise and bring extra oil for their lamps, while the other five are foolish and do not bring any extra oil.

Seizing Opportunities: Why Preparation is Key to Success

When the bridegroom becomes delayed, all ten virgins fall asleep. When the bridegroom finally arrives, the five foolish virgins realize they do not have enough oil to burn in their lamps. In comparison, the five wise virgins have plenty of oil. The foolish virgins then ask the wise virgins for some of their oil, but they refuse, telling the foolish virgins to go and buy oil for themselves.

While the foolish virgins are out buying oil, the bridegroom arrives, and the five wise virgins enter the wedding banquet with him. When the foolish virgins return, they find they have missed the wedding banquet and are not allowed to enter.

This story is often interpreted, and rightly so, as a lesson about being prepared for the return of Jesus and the need always to be spiritually ready. But we can draw further lessons on the importance of personal responsibility and the consequences of failing to be prepared for important events and opportunities.

When I have conversations with people and they are quick to criticize a government administration, I often ask this question: "What would you do differently if allowed to lead?" The responses are mainly in the lines, "Let me get there first, and you'd see what I'd do." Once I hear a comment like this, I know I am speaking to someone unprepared for future opportunities. Don't wait for an opportunity before you figure out what to do with it. You must always be ready to show what you can do first, and then opportunities for demonstrations will follow.

Another variation is when people talk about wishing they would magically get a large sum of money. And then I ask, "What would you do with the money if you get it." And then comes the response, "Wait until I get it, and you'll see what I'd do with it."

Don't wait for an opportunity before you figure out what to do with it.

In 2022, shortly before the Nigerian presidential election of 2023, the Central Bank of Nigeria (CBN) launched a redesign of some naira notes. As part of the redesign process, the CBN announced that it would be recalling the old banknotes and replacing them with new ones. This announcement led to a rush by Nigerians to exchange the old banknotes for the new ones. Reports emerged of people discovering caches of old banknotes buried in the ground, at home, or at other locations. Burying money just shows you how people can have money and not know what to do with it; they bury it in the ground. Does this remind you of the servant who buried the talent his master gave

Seizing Opportunities: Why Preparation is Key to Success

him because he didn't know what to do with it? (Matthew 25: 14-30). Many people today assume they'd be better off with a lot of money, so they engage in an endless quest to acquire lots of it. And once they have it, they don't know what to do with it.

In 2009, the ABC Network premiered the TV show "Shark Tank'' in the United States. "Shark Tank" is a reality television show where entrepreneurs and small business owners pitch their ideas to a panel of successful businesspeople, or "sharks," in the hopes of securing an investment. What I love about "Shark Tank" is that it is a platform that provides the right place and time for entrepreneurs who are prepared to take advantage of the opportunities the show offers. The entrepreneurs present their ideas, demonstrate their products or services, and provide financial information to the sharks. The sharks then ask questions and make offers to invest in the business in exchange for a percentage of ownership. The entrepreneurs can then choose to accept or decline the offers. The show is strategically designed to provide a platform for entrepreneurs to showcase their businesses and potentially secure funding while also providing entertainment for viewers. It's a popular show, airing in different countries, and the sharks are usually successful entrepreneurs or investors looking to invest in new business opportunities.

One of the show's elements is for the sharks to question the entrepreneurs to decipher their preparedness and what they'd do with the money they requested. Can you imagine how absurd it would be for an entrepreneur to say, "I don't know what I would do with the money yet, but I want you to trust me and give me the money, and you'll see what I'd do with it when I have it." Nobody would invest in a person like that. I know some people think that God throws His resources around to people and then waits to see what they'd do with them, but that is not the way of God. Instead, God commits His resources to individuals according to their abilities and preparedness to handle those resources. You must be prepared for opportunities so that you won't have regrets like the story of the foolish virgins for whom it was the right time and opportunity, yet they were not prepared.

Time and Chance

> "I have observed something else under the sun. The fastest runner doesn't always win the race, and the strongest warrior doesn't always win the battle. The wise sometimes go hungry, and the skillful are not necessarily wealthy. And those who are educated don't always lead successful lives. It is all decided by chance, by being in the

right place at the right time."

Ecclesiastes 9:11 NLT.

Suppose you have ever lived internationally apart from your loved ones. In that case, you understand the difficulty of frequent communications, primarily due to the high cost of making international calls. As a result, the need for a very cost-effective way of communicating frequently becomes necessary. The need for a cost-effective means of communication is where an app like WhatsApp comes in.

Jan Koum, one of the co-founders of WhatsApp, came to the United States from Ukraine with his mother to escape anti-Semitic violence and persecution. Despite their hardship, Koum excelled in school and eventually landed a job as an infrastructure engineer at Yahoo.

After leaving Yahoo in 2007, Koum and his business partner, Brian Acton, took a year off to travel to South America. After they returned to the United States, they started considering joining another company or starting their own. Jan Koum conceived the idea of enhancing user experience with the emergence of new technologies like Skype. The inspiration for this was from his teenage years when costly communication made contact irregular with his family. His aim was to create a user-friendly, cross-platform messaging app that would make phone calls and text more accessible to those facing similar challenges with communication. This was the idea that led to the creation of WhatsApp. WhatsApp would become a messaging app that would allow people to communicate for free, regardless of their location or financial situation.

WhatsApp was officially launched in 2009, but it struggled so much initially to gain traction that Koum and Acton had to survive on their savings while continuing to develop the app.

It wasn't until 2011, when Apple launched iMessage, which validated the idea of free messaging apps and created a market, that WhatsApp's fortunes began to change. The launch of iMessage was the perfect timing for Koum and Acton to capitalize on the opportunity and take their app to the next level. They were prepared to take advantage of this opportunity and pivot their business model to focus on growth and user acquisition.

Their ability to recognize the opportunity and pivot their business model was crucial to the success of WhatsApp. They were in the right place at the right time and prepared to take advantage of the opportunity.

In 2014, Facebook acquired WhatsApp for $19 billion, making Koum and Acton billionaires. Today, WhatsApp

Seizing Opportunities: Why Preparation is Key to Success

has over 2 billion monthly active users and has become one of the most popular messaging apps in the world.

The story of WhatsApp and Koum's journey is about being at the right place at the right time and being adequately prepared to take advantage of opportunities when they arise. Koum's personal experience of struggling to stay in touch with his family members because of the high cost of international calls was the inspiration for WhatsApp and ultimately gave him the vision that led to the creation of a product that has changed the way people communicate and has become an essential part of our lives today.

****

King Solomon in the Bible received unparalleled wisdom, riches, and honor from God. The Queen of Sheba came to Solomon with difficult questions after she heard of his fame. During their meeting, "…she talked with him about everything she had on her mind. Solomon had answers for all her questions; nothing was too hard for him to explain to her." Seeing first-hand the wisdom of Solomon on display took the Queen's breath away. She later admitted that the wisdom of Solomon was far beyond what she was told. (2 Chronicles 9:1-7 NLT)

The Bible said of Solomon that he "could speak with

authority about all kinds of plants, from the great cedar of Lebanon to the tiny hyssop that grows from cracks in a wall. He could also speak about animals, birds, small creatures, and fish." (1 Kings 4:33 NLT)

This Bible verse means Solomon could make grandiose plans and strategies. He is someone who could see the bigger picture and discuss how the minor details fit.

This same Solomon, in all his wisdom, was the one who concluded thus about success:

> "I have observed something else under the sun. The fastest runner doesn't always win the race, and the strongest warrior doesn't always win the battle. The wise sometimes go hungry, and the skillful are not necessarily wealthy. And those who are educated don't always lead successful lives. *It is all decided by chance, by being in the right place at the right time."*
> **Ecclesiastes 9:11 NLT (emphasis mine).**

When you think of success or successful people, what comes to mind, or what major attribute would you ascribe to their success? Speed, strength, wisdom, skills? Are these not what we look for in successful people? He is faster than most people. He is stronger, wiser, and the most

Seizing Opportunities: Why Preparation is Key to Success

skillful. After all his careful observations and reflections, King Solomon concluded that success is not just about all of these but also about being in the right place at the right time. You can have all the so-called attributes of success - swiftness, strength, wisdom, understanding, skills, and education - but it can mean nothing if you are not in the right place at the right time.

The point here is that success is about the time you have, the circumstances surrounding you, and the opportunities you see and maximize. Success is a unique combination of having the right opportunities presented to you and being at the right place and time to capitalize on those opportunities. However, what enables you to capitalize on those opportunities is the level of your preparedness before the opportunities arrive.

In 2008, Malcolm Gladwell published his famous book, *Outliers: The Story of Success*. In *Outliers*, Gladwell examines the factors that contribute to high levels of success. He argues that "in examining the lives of the remarkable among us – the skilled, the talented, and the driven, … there is something profoundly wrong with the way we make sense of success." Drawing from numerous examples, Gladwell concluded that "people don't rise from nothing." Instead, the time a person is born, including the environment, upbringing, and opportunities that exist because of those elements, all determine the trajectory of that person's life. Successful people were born at unique times and seasons. Because of this, they were placed in situations that enabled them to put in an extraordinary amount of work in preparing for future possibilities.

> Success is a unique combination of having the right opportunities presented to you and being at the right place and time to capitalize on those opportunities.

"Success is not a random act. It arises out of a predictable and powerful set of circumstances and opportunities." (*The Outlier,* Malcolm Gladwell) Nevertheless, you must be prepared for those opportunities before they come so that when they come, you'll have a head start in the game. Successful people were given unique opportunities to work hard, and they seized it. They happened to come of age when that extraordinary effort was rewarded by society.

****

> *"It is not often that a man can make opportunities for himself. But he can put himself in such shape that when or if the opportunities come, he is ready."*
>
> **Theodore Roosevelt**

While you cannot control the time and circumstances in which you were born, you have some control over how you can prepare and get yourself ready for the future. You have unique talents, skills, and abilities that can be developed and honed over time. You may not be able to predict the future with absolute certainty, but you can take steps to be better prepared for what may come. Ultimately, the choices you make today can have a significant impact on your future. You can position yourself for success and be better prepared to navigate whatever challenges and opportunities the future may bring.

You may now be wondering: how do I know what to start preparing for? Things are changing at dizzying speed, and skills that are cultivated today may be irrelevant tomorrow. How do I know what I should start preparing for today that would earn me commercial value tomorrow or position me for success? The answers to these questions are the subject of the next chapter.

Prayers

1. Pray that you will be ready when opportunities come knocking on your door.

2. Pray that God will grant you supernatural focus on the right opportunities and how to be adequately prepared for them.

3. Pray for wisdom and strength that you need to ensure your adequate preparation.

Confession

I declare that I am positioned strategically for unique opportunities and favors. I am always at the right place and time. I am prepared to navigate whatever challenges and opportunities the future may bring.

Reflective Questions

1. What are some of the areas of your life that you need to focus on preparing for the future?

2. What steps can you take to identify areas in which you should start preparing for the future, considering the rapidly changing world and evolving skill requirements?

3. How much do you trust God to help you prepare for the future?

4. How can you use your gifts and talents to make a positive impact on the future?

Seizing Opportunities: Why Preparation is Key to Success

Action Note

Please use this section to write down things you will start doing based on what you have learned in this chapter.

_____
_____
_____
_____
_____
_____
_____
_____
_____
_____
_____
_____
_____
_____
_____
_____
_____
_____
_____
_____

CHAPTER 2

Building Your Boats

"In times of change, learners inherit the earth, while the learned find themselves beautifully equipped to deal with a world that no longer exists."

- **Eric Hoffer**

In early February 2020, I was working in an office when I overheard one of my colleagues screaming and yelling. I approached her to ask what was wrong, and she pointed to the TV screen where people were wearing masks as a precaution against the COVID-19 virus that was beginning to spread.

My colleague remained skeptical despite my attempts to explain why these measures were necessary. "Seeing people wearing masks gives me anxiety," she said. She also felt like people were exaggerating the imminence of the spread of the virus. Little did we know that the COVID-19 pandemic would become a reality that would impact our lives for several months.

As the situation escalated, panic began, and people rushed to stock up on groceries and essential supplies. Unfortunately, many of these measures came too late to prevent the spread of the virus.

In the case of the COVID-19 pandemic, many people were caught off guard by the rapid spread of the virus and its resulting disruptions to daily life.

The COVID-19 pandemic created a lot of uncertainty and made it difficult for people to plan for the future. Many individuals and organizations had to adapt quickly to the changing circumstances and prepare for something that had not happened before.

One example of this is the shift to remote work. With many offices and workplaces closing to prevent the spread of the virus, employees had to quickly transition to working from home. Working from home required significant preparation, including setting up home offices, purchasing necessary equipment and software, and adjusting to new communication and collaboration tools.

****

Zoom Video Communications, Inc. was founded in 2011 by a former Cisco Webex engineer Eric Yuan. The company started as a video conferencing software designed for businesses and organizations, focusing on providing a user-friendly and reliable platform.

Before the COVID-19 pandemic, Zoom had already experienced steady growth and had established itself as a leading video conferencing software. However, with the onset of the pandemic, Zoom experienced massive growth and became an essential tool for remote work and online learning.

One reason for Zoom's success during the pandemic was its prior preparation and investment in the technology and infrastructure needed to support high-quality video conferencing. In the years leading up to the pandemic, Zoom had invested heavily in cloud infrastructure and developed a scalable and reliable platform to accommodate large groups of people.

Additionally, Zoom had focused on creating a user-friendly and intuitive interface, which made it easy for people to use and adopt. This prior preparation and investment in technology and user experience gave Zoom a competitive advantage when the pandemic hit.

As the pandemic spread, Zoom's user base grew exponentially. Businesses, schools, and organizations worldwide turned to Zoom as a reliable and user-friendly platform for remote communication and collaboration.

Additionally, individuals and families began using Zoom for virtual socializing and events, further expanding its customer base.

To keep up with the increased demand, Zoom quickly adapted and added new features to its platform, such as virtual backgrounds and enhanced security measures. The company also offered free access to its platform for schools and provided resources and support for educators.

As a result of its preparation and innovation, Zoom experienced massive growth during the COVID-19 pandemic. Its revenue and profits increased dramatically, and its stock price skyrocketed. While the pandemic created uncertainty and challenges for many businesses, Zoom's prior preparation and investment positioned it for massive opportunities and success.

By Faith

I believe these examples have convinced you of the need to prepare adequately for unique challenges and opportunities that you may not be aware of in the present. But you may also be wondering how you can begin preparing for an unknown and uncertain future so that you are prepared and ready when the time comes. The short answer is, by faith!

Hebrews 11:1 (NKJV) says,

> "Now faith is the substance of things hoped for, the evidence of things not seen."

There is faith for healing, there is faith for prosperity, there is the faith that secures our salvation, etc. There is also faith that enables us to prepare for the future. Whenever we are dealing in the realm of things that are not observable to our physical senses or something we expect to happen, we need faith in operation, because to have faith is to be sure of what we cannot see. That certainty is what enables us to prepare with confidence.

My wife and I marked our first wedding anniversary by going to Puerto Rico. During our flight, we looked out the window and were captivated by the striking sight of the magnificent mountains. From the window, you could see the sky, the mountains, the land, and the sea. A stunning rainbow appeared in the sky adding to the incredible scenery. Of course, we have both seen rainbows many times before. However, this one felt special; perhaps the joy and excitement of our first anniversary trip made everything look and feel special. Also, the heightened altitude and breathtaking surroundings possibly added to the rainbow's beauty.

As we admired the beauty before us, my wife turned to me and shared what she had been thinking. "Whenever I see a rainbow, it reminds me of Noah's story and the covenant God made with him after the flood," she said. To put this in context, let us briefly examine what happened before God made this covenant with Noah.

As told in Genesis chapters 6 and 7, the story begins with God becoming disillusioned with humanity's wickedness and deciding to flood the earth to start anew. God selects Noah, a righteous man, to build an ark and save himself, his family, and a pair of every kind of animal from the impending flood.

Noah obediently constructs the ark, and once completed, he loads it with the animals and his family. As the rain begins to fall, the waters of the flood start to rise until they eventually cover the earth, wiping out all living beings except those on the ark.

After 40 days and nights of rainfall, the flood subsides, and Noah sends a dove to search for dry land. The dove returns with an olive leaf, indicating that the waters have receded, and the ark eventually comes to rest on a mountain. Noah and his family disembark and offer sacrifices to God in gratitude for their survival.

In response to Noah's faithfulness, God makes a covenant never to destroy all living creatures with a flood again and creates the rainbow as a symbol of the covenant.

This story offers several valuable lessons for every believer in our world today. It reminds us that sin has consequences and that we must be mindful of our actions and their impact on others. The story also shows the importance of obeying God's commands, even when they seem difficult or impractical. We can also see God's mercy and grace in action here and that God is not just a God of judgment, but also a God of mercy and grace.

However, I like to emphasize the importance of faith and the lessons we can draw from it to help us prepare for future unforeseen events.

God is revealed as a Spirit who delights in revealing plans and what will happen in the future to His people, giving them instructions on how to prepare for those events and occurrences in a way that would save them and their loved ones. Let's take a deeper look to see some faith principles in action.

> "*By faith* Noah, being *divinely warned* of
> *things not yet seen*, moved with godly fear,
> *prepared* an ark for the *saving* of his household,
> by which he condemned the world and became

heir of the righteousness which is according to faith."

Hebrews 11:7 NKJV (emphasis mine)

By Faith:

"And Noah did according to all that the LORD commanded him."

Genesis 7:5 (NKJV)

Faith, defined, is the response of the human spirit to the Word of God. That means your heart receives a word from God and then you act on it. As we can see from Hebrews 11:7, Noah acted, following what God commanded him. His obedience is ultimately rooted in his faith in God. He trusts that God will keep His promises and protect him and his family. His faith in God prompted Noah's action. The construction of an ark for an event that had never happened on earth before was Noah's response to what God told him about the future.

Warned by God:

Noah's actions were not based on his human impulses or calculations. Instead, they were based on what God told him would happen. The sure foundation of our faith is the Word of God. To step out in faith is to have the Word of God as the foundation for our subsequent actions. So many people assume faith is a determination to get something done or achieve something. They fail to realize that acting in faith means you have gotten a prior word from God about what to do in your situation or circumstance. Without the Word of God backing your actions, you will be acting presumptuously.

Events Not Seen:

You can imagine how ridiculous it must be to work on something no one has ever experienced. Our minds are comfortable doing routine things. But the core of our faith is about things not yet experienced by our physical senses. It is faith because you are expecting something that is not yet seen; it is "the evidence of things not seen" (Hebrews 11:1 NKJV). Faith is about a future state that you believe will happen and that you are expecting because God said so. You can know faith by the certainty of an expectancy for something not yet seen. To be sure that something that is not yet seen will happen based on the word of God is a high level of faith. When something is within the perception of your physical senses, then you don't need faith for it.

> Faith is about a future state that you believe
> will happen and that you are expecting
> because God said so.

"For we were saved in this hope, but hope that is seen is not hope; for why does one still hope for what he sees? But if we hope for what we do not see, we eagerly wait for it with perseverance."

Romans 8:24-25 NKJV

Prepared:

The reason God reveals events not seen to us is so that we can prepare for them now.

One biblical example that illustrates the importance of being prepared for future trends is the story of Joseph in the book of Genesis. Joseph was sold into slavery by his brothers and taken to Egypt. In Egypt, he was falsely accused and subsequently thrown into prison.

While in prison, Joseph interpreted the dreams of some of his prison mates: a butler and a baker. The butler was restored to his initial position in the palace to fulfill his interpreted dream. The chief baker, on the other hand, was hanged according to the interpretation of Joseph. Then after a while, Pharaoh, king of Egypt, also had two dreams that proved difficult for everyone around him to interpret. In his first dream, he was by the river and saw seven fine-looking and well-fed cows feeding by the meadow. Then he saw another seven cows, ugly and gaunt, that appeared and ate up the seven fine-looking and fat cows. In his second dream, he saw seven heads of grain, plump and good. And then seven thin heads came up after them. The seven thin heads of grain devoured the seven plump and full heads. Joseph was then called upon to interpret the king's dream.

Joseph interpreted the dream as the foretelling of unforeseen events, in this case, seven years of famine to be preceded by seven years of plenty. He then suggested that the country prepare for the coming famine by storing grain during the years of plenty. Pharaoh heeded Joseph's advice and installed him as prime minister. As a result, Egypt was able to survive the famine that followed.

When God shows you things to come, you must prepare for them. "Faith without works is dead." (James 2:17 NKJV). The works referred to in this verse means corresponding actions. Faith without corresponding actions will not work. Imagine Noah saying that he believes what God told him is true and that the earth would genuinely experience its first ever flood, but not taking actions to prepare for what is to come. That would have been highly ridiculous. So, you see, our corresponding action gives life to our faith.

Saving:

According to Genesis 7:12, it rained for forty days and forty nights. The water increased and lifted the ark, and it rose above the earth. The flood destroyed all living things on the face of the ground, both man and cattle, creeping things, and birds of the air. Only Noah and those who were with him in the ark remained alive.

When you follow God's instructions, the situations and conditions that destroy others will be the same factors that will lift you.

God's ultimate plan is to give you a pleasant future, to save you and all that belongs to you. The revelation of His plans to you is so that you can make preparations that would result in your salvation.

In the New Testament, the word salvation does not only refer to the salvation that takes us to heaven. In this verse, the word saving means physical or moral rescue or safety. It also connotes deliverance, healing, salvation, and safety.

So, we can summarize the story of Noah thus: Noah was divinely warned by God of things not yet seen by anyone living on earth. Noah believed the Word of God and responded in faith by preparing an ark that ultimately saved him and his entire household.

> When you follow God's instructions,
> the situations and conditions that
> destroy others will be the same
> factors that will lift you.

A modern person might say, "How is the story of the flood relevant today?" Noah's faith in God to prepare a boat according to God's instructions is more suitable to the unique circumstances and situation of his days. However, the major lessons from the story are still applicable today. You may not be getting instructions to build a boat like Noah, but there may be other areas for which God is giving you instructions. In your case, it could be to start a business, get a particular degree, start your ministry, invest in certain areas, etc. You might not see the need at the time, but if you heed the call, you might be building your own boat that will be for the saving of yourself and your family.

Preparing for the Future: Three Essential Steps

> "The secret of success in life is for a man to be ready for his opportunity when it comes."
> — **Benjamin Disraeli**

Ian Abrams, Patrick Q. Page, and Vik Rubenfeld created a TV show produced by CBS Productions and aired from 1996 to 2000 called "Early Edition." The show starred Kyle Chandler as Gary Hobson, a man who receives tomorrow's newspaper today and tries to prevent bad things from happening. The show's premise was that a mysterious cat would deliver a newspaper to Hobson every morning, containing news events that would occur the following day. Hobson would then try to prevent or alter the events described in the newspaper, often with the help of his friends Chuck Fishman (played by Fisher Stevens) and Marissa Clark (played by Shanesia Davis-Williams). The show focuses on Hobson's attempts to use his foreknowledge of events to help others.

Hobson knew what was coming because he got the future handed to him in advance. He knew what he needed to do in light of what the newspaper said would happen the next day because he got it ahead of time.

Can you imagine knowing what is coming because the knowledge of the future is given to you in advance? Not only that, but you also know what you need to do today to prepare for what is to come tomorrow.

Throughout the Bible, God, using diverse means, is seen as always showing His people what will happen and what they can do in preparation for the future. Prophecy is God's newspaper, telling you what's coming tomorrow so you have the information today.

Many people today find themselves facing a wide range of choices and challenges when it comes to planning their future. Admittedly, the lack of clear guidance and direction can be daunting. For one, having this kind of insider information would be nice because foresight into what will happen in the future can be an incredibly valuable tool that can help you better prepare for various aspects of life. Imagine how productive your life would become if you knew what was coming tomorrow. This knowledge would make you better equipped to make the right decisions in your personal lives.

For instance, take the educational sector, where students are being prepared for jobs that no longer exist. Educational institutions face challenges in providing students with skills that will remain relevant in the future. Educators can't keep up with changing dynamics and rapid technological advancement. In this instance, the challenge of choosing the right degree or educational path can be a significant source of uncertainty for many people. There are so many options available, from traditional four-year degrees to vocational training and online courses, that it can be challenging to know what kind of education will be most valuable in the long run. And with the cost of education continuing to rise, the stakes are higher than ever when it comes to making the right choice.

Technology continues to disrupt the workforce, changing the skills that will be relevant in the future and kind of jobs that will be available. Therefore, you can rightly question if the popular college degrees we know and speak of today will still be relevant in the next ten to twenty years. But if we know which skills will be in high demand in the years to come, we can ensure we're learning and practicing those skills now. Also, if we know that a certain degree or certification will be required for a particular job in the future, we can start working towards that goal early on.

The same logic applies when making the right career or business decision. Knowing what's coming can help you make better decisions about your career paths. Knowing what job markets will be in demand in the future can help you make informed decisions about what kind of education and training will be needed to be competitive.

The good news is that you can depend on God for insights into tomorrow that would allow you to begin preparations today for tomorrow's opportunities. God delights in revealing things to His children. I will now share three essential steps that can help you with this.

Step 1: He Tells You His Plan

> "Indeed, the Sovereign Lord never does anything until he reveals his plans to his servants the prophets."
>
> **Amos 3:7 NLT**

> "Whatever the LORD God plans to do, he tells his servants, the prophets."
>
> **Amos 3:7 CEV**

One frequently asked question among modern Christians is, "How do I know God's plan and purpose for my life?" And most times, the answers provided are unnecessarily complex processes that leave people even more confused and in doubt. But that is not the evidence from scriptures. It is a common theme in scripture for God to reveal His plans and purposes to human beings. I am often fascinated by how God would tell people what He intends to do before carrying it out, as though He needs permission or approval. God announced the plan for man's redemption and was massively proclaimed by His prophets long before the actual act of redemption. In Genesis Chapter 18, God informs Abraham of His plans before the destruction of Sodom. God says, "Shall I hide what I am doing from Abraham?" Hezekiah is another example in the Bible. God sent the prophet Isaiah to announce to him that he would die. Hezekiah prayed to God for mercy and God answered his prayers by adding fifteen more years to his life. If God intended for Hezekiah to die, why send a warning? A story like this leaves me wondering if God intended for Hezekiah to die or if God was looking for someone to restrain him.

The point here is that God reveals His plans to His people even before He executes them. And for you as an individual, God has a plan for the best outcomes for your life, and He delights in revealing those plans to you.

> "'For I know the plans I have for you,' says the Lord. 'They are plans for good and not for disaster, to give you a future and a hope.'"
>
> **Jeremiah 29:11 NLT**

Looking back again to the story of Noah, we see that "by faith Noah was divinely warned of things not yet seen." In other words, he got insights into things to come. As a believer, your significant advantage in life is that you have the Holy Spirit inside of you. And one of the works of the Holy Spirit, according to Jesus, is that the Holy Spirit will tell you of things to come.

> "But when He, the Spirit of Truth (the Truth-giving Spirit) comes, He will guide you into all the Truth (the whole, full Truth). For He will not speak His own message (on His own authority]; but He will tell whatever He hears [from the Father; He will give the message that has been given to Him], and he will announce and declare to you the things that are to come [that will happen in the future].
>
> **John 16:13 AMPC**

Amazing! *"The Holy Spirit will declare to you the things to come, things that will happen in the future."* He takes the conversations in heaven between the Father and the Son and then reveals to you what pertains to your life and future. Think about this for a while and let it sink into your spirit. Perhaps your lack of awareness of this truth is why you have not been taking advantage of this great revelation. But now that you are aware, focus on this thought for a while. Amid the chaos of life and all the uncertainty about the future, your career, your education, your business, your finance, your ministry, you can believe God for the revelations of things to come, especially concerning your future.

If God has a plan for you and your future and delights to reveal those plans to you, then you can begin this journey by asking Him to reveal them to you.

In Jeremiah 33:3 NLT, God says, "Ask me and I will tell you remarkable secrets you do not know about *things to come*" (emphasis mine).

Here are some prayers and confessions to help you get started.

PRAYERS

1. Thank God for His unique and excellent plans for your life that guarantee a great future and hope for you.

2. Pray to God that His Spirit will reveal what will come in your life. Ask the Holy Spirit to show you God's secrets concerning your life. Ask Him to reveal what God has planned for you, especially now.

3. Ask God to grant you insight and understanding and that He instructs you and helps you gain wisdom.

4. Pray that His plans are known to you and that He gives you the wisdom to know what steps you need to take to fulfill them.

CONFESSION

As it is written, "Eye has not seen, nor ear heard, nor have entered into the heart of man the things which God has prepared for those who love Him." (1 Corinthians 2:9 NKJV)

These things are revealed to me. I come into a conscious awareness of them. I know of technological trends, market forces, and future opportunities shaping the world. I am rightly positioned for unique opportunities and well prepared to take advantage of them.

Step 2: He Tells You What to Do

> "The Lord says, 'I will guide you along the best pathway for your life. I will advise you and watch over you.'"
>
> **Psalm 32:8 NLT**

God has a plan for your future and delights in revealing those plans to you. You can start to trust God to show you things yet to come in your future so that you can position yourself adequately to maximize every opportunity. But there is more. God also wants to show you what to do and how to go about His plans. Remember, He knows the best route to get you to your assigned destination and the purpose for His plan's revelations is to prepare you for what is yet to come.

Let us go back to the story of Noah. First, God revealed His plans for the earth to him. Second, God initiated the next step and instructed Noah on what to do to preserve himself and his family when the time came for His plan to be executed. He told Noah, "Make yourself an ark of gopherwood; make rooms in the ark and cover it inside and outside with pitch." (Genesis 6:14 NKJV).

Here you can see the difference between information and insight. You can have information about something and still not know what to do about it. The internet has a lot of information about almost everything on earth. And with the rapid pace of internet penetration worldwide, it means even people in remote villages access powerful information. But what makes a difference is not the amount of information you have, but how you can make sense of the information. Noah knew what would happen in the future, but what would he do with that information? Information is useless when it is not followed by a specific knowledge of what to do with it. Knowing what to do about a particular piece of information is called insight. The Bible described the sons of Issachar as being distinguished from their brethren because they knew what Israel ought to do. In this current world, something that can give you an edge is when you can tell people what to do based on the information you have. Companies, organizations, and individuals are making huge fortunes just by interpreting information and giving insights into what to do based on the current trends being observed.

> Information is useless when it is not followed by a specific knowledge of what to do with it.

The instruction to build an ark is a specific instruction about what to do with the information God revealed to Noah – make an ark.

God didn't just help Noah make sense of the information, but He also instructed Noah on how to make the ark. Often, believers hear something from God and quickly run with it. But when God shares any information with you, make sure you stay with Him long enough to know and understand what you can do with that information. God told

Noah, "And this is how you shall make it: The length of the ark shall be three hundred cubits, its width fifty cubits, and its height thirty cubits. You shall make a window for the ark, and you shall finish it to a cubit from above; and set the door of the ark in the side. You shall make it with lower, second, and third decks" (Genesis 6:15-16 NKJV).

God gave Noah specific details on how to prepare the ark because He knew the intricacies of what would happen and what would be needed in every particular instance.

To have an advantage in the future, you need revelatory insights into what you should start doing now and how to do it.

PRAYERS

1. Thank God for the spirit of insight and understanding into great revelations.

2. Ask God to help you make sense of and understand what to do with the information that you have.

3. Pray to God for revelatory insights into what you should start doing today and how you should go about it.

CONFESSION

The Spirit of God is leading and guiding me in the ways

I should go. By divine power, I am instructed on what to do in my life, family, career, and business. I also have instructions on how to do them.

Step 3: Step Out in Faith

Once you have received a revelation of God's plan and instructions about what to do and how to do it, the next crucial step is to take a leap of faith and prepare for what God has warned or instructed you about.

Sometimes, your current situation may make it seem like you don't need to start preparing for something significant, much like Noah's community didn't require an ark. Think about it: before the Flood of Noah, there was no account of rain on the earth. According to the creation account in Genesis 2:5-6 (NKJV), before the creation of man, the land was watered by a mist that went up from the earth for the Lord God had not caused it to rain on the earth. And then in Genesis Chapter 7 and 8 the Flood came which is often interpreted as a cataclysmic event that reshaped the Earth's climate and topography. It was at this time that Noah was instructed to prepare an ark. Alternatively, the preparation that you need to undertake may seem unrelated to your present circumstances. However, it is crucial to understand that God is not preparing you merely for what you have seen and undergone. Instead, He is preparing you for what is yet to come, something you may not even be aware of yet; this, my friend, requires faith.

> No human mind has ever thought of what God has prepared for you.

"However, as it is written: 'What no eye has seen, what no ear has heard, and what no human mind has conceived' - the things God has prepared for those who love him - these are the things God has revealed to us by His Spirit. The Spirit searches all things, even the deep things of God." (1 Corinthians 2:9-10 NKJV) Anytime I read this scripture, it just blows my mind away. I want you to understand that no human mind has ever thought of what God has prepared for you. That means, what God has prepared for you has never been done by anyone else. The plan He has for you is original and you will have to depend totally on Him for the revelation and execution of that plan. What is even far more interesting is that what no human mind has ever conceived, the Bible in this verse says that those are the things that the Holy Spirit reveals to us.

> "When the seventh angel blows his trumpet, God's mysterious plan will be fulfilled. *It will happen just as he announced it to his servants the prophets.*"
> **Revelation 10:7 NLT (emphasis mine).**

Build your boats before the floodwater comes

When God announces His plan, you shouldn't second guess if it will happen, because it will happen exactly as He announced it. If you step out in faith, it will happen just as He told you. Every minute detail will come to pass just as He said it would. You don't want to meet with specific challenges today that God had already instructed you about years ago. Neither do you want to meet with challenges in the future that God is giving you revelations about today. Imagine Noah starting to prepare the ark when the flood was already on the earth. The principle here is straightforward: build your boats before the floodwater comes.

PRAYERS

1. Pray that the Lord grants you the ability to prepare now for things that society will be rewarding in the coming years.

2. Ask the Father to give you the strength and courage to act on all His divine instructions and commands.

3. Pray that God will help you avoid every harmful distraction that may tempt you away from doing the things God is instructing you on.

CONFESSION

In the name of Jesus, I am empowered to act on the insights and instructions that the Lord reveals to me. As I take steps on them, I am rightly positioned to receive and benefit from all God had planned for me beforehand.

Reflective Questions

1. In what specific areas do you think God is calling you today to start building your boats?

2. What are the main issues you can identify that are holding you back from taking steps in the direction that God is revealing to you?

3. Reflect on a time when you received a strong sense of divine guidance or instruction. What was your initial response, and what did you learn from that experience?

4. Consider the notion that faith can inspire you to take actions today, even when the future outcomes are uncertain. How does this perspective influence your approach to life and decision-making?

5. In your own faith journey, can you identify moments when you were called to "build your boats" by taking proactive steps, trusting that these actions would serve your advantage in the future?

Action Note

Please use this section to write down things you will start doing based on what you have learned in this chapter.

CHAPTER 3

Breaking Through Limitations: Overcoming Systems and Structures

"You have to act as if it were possible to radically transform the world. And you have to do it all the time."

Angela Davis

James McHenry, a Black veteran, returned to Baltimore after serving in World War II. Like many black veterans, McHenry was eager to take advantage of the GI Bill and purchase a home for his family. He soon discovered that the discrimination he had experienced while serving his country was not limited to the military.

In Baltimore, he found that he and other Black veterans were effectively shut out of the mainstream housing market. Banks and insurance companies refused to provide mortgages or insurance in Black neighborhoods, making it nearly impossible for Black residents to purchase homes. This led to a "Black market" for housing, where Black residents were forced to pay exorbitant rents and live in substandard conditions.

Despite these challenges, McHenry was determined to own a home. He eventually found a home in a Black neighborhood on the west side of Baltimore, where he had to pay much more than a White person would have for a similar home in a White neighborhood. He also had to pay cash for the home, as he could not get a mortgage.

****

This practice, where banks, real estate agents, and other lending institutions refuse to provide loans or other financial services to people in specific neighborhoods based on the racial or ethnic makeup of those neighborhoods, is called *redlining*. The term "redlining" comes from drawing red lines on maps to indicate areas where loans would not be given, or insurance would not be sold. Redlining has historically been used to discriminate against people of color, keeping them from buying homes and accumulating wealth.

The Federal Housing Administration (FHA) and the Home Owners' Loan Corporation (HOLC) in the United States during the 1930s and 1940s used a system of maps and ratings to determine which neighborhoods were eligible for government-backed mortgages. Communities with a high proportion of minority residents were often given the lowest ratings and labeled as "hazardous" or "definitely declining." This meant that residents in those neighborhoods were effectively shut out of the government-backed mortgage market, which made it much harder for them to buy homes and accumulate wealth.

Thankfully, redlining was officially banned by the Fair Housing Act of 1968; however, the effects are still felt in some areas where the practice is common.

Redlining is just one of many systems and structures that are designed to keep a specific group of people from accessing wealth-building opportunities.

The Wall of Jericho

The story of the Wall of Jericho is a classic biblical example of a built structure that was effectively utilized to keep a particular class of people out. The wall was a fortification that surrounded the ancient city of Jericho. To understand this story, we must start with the book of Genesis. In Genesis, God promised Abraham that his descendants would inherit a land flowing with milk and honey, later known as the Promised Land (Canaan). This promise was then passed down to Isaac, Jacob, and their descendants, who became the children of Israel.

Before the Israelites could occupy the Promised Land,

the Egyptians enslaved them for several centuries. God then raised Moses to lead the Israelites out of slavery and toward the Promised Land. Moses led them through the wilderness for forty years before he died and was succeeded by his assistant, Joshua. "After the death of Moses, the servant of the LORD, it came to pass that the LORD spoke to Joshua the son of Nun, Moses' assistant, saying: Moses My servant is dead. Now therefore, arise, go over this Jordan, you and all this people, to the land which I am giving to them – the children of Israel." Joshua 1:1-2 NKJV.

Under the Lord's direction and the leadership of Joshua, the children of Israel began a gradual conquest of Canaan (the Promised Land) and began to take possession of the land. In this quest, the first city in Israel's way was Jericho, the natural place for the Israelites to enter the Promised Land. To conquer Jericho, Joshua sent spies to investigate the city. The spies lodged at the house of a harlot named Rahab, who knew Israel would overthrow Jericho. Thus, she hid the spies and later helped them escape on the promise that Israel would spare her and her family when they took over the city.

The inhabitants of Jericho also feared the children of Israel because they heard of all the exploits and conquests of the Israelites after they left Egypt. So, as soon as they learned that the Israelites were close to Jericho, they took measures to keep them out.

> "Now Jericho was securely shut up because of the children of Israel; none went out, and none came in."
>
> **Joshua 6:1**

To prevent Israel from entering Jericho, the people of Jericho utilized their well-known system of fortress – the wall. It was so effective that nobody could go in. Also equally important is that nobody could go out. It is a system designed to preserve the status quo.

Therefore, to enter the promise of God, the Israelites had to contend with the wall of Jericho, which was strategically designed to keep them out. According to archaeological research, the city walls were constructed around 8000 BCE and were made of mud bricks reinforced with straw. The wall was about 3.6 meters (12 feet) high and about 1.8 meters (6 feet) thick. The wall was intended to protect the settlement and its water supply from human intruders. It suffices to say that the Wall of Jericho was a formidable obstacle for any invading army, and the Israelites, who were trying to conquer the city, faced this difficult task.

The wall of Jericho represented a formidable physical barrier that stood as an obstacle to the Israelites' entry into the Promised Land. However, despite being well-fortified, the wall eventually fell, tumbling like a house of cards. The people of Jericho were stunned, unable to comprehend what was happening before their eyes.

Today, the chances of facing a physical barrier in the form of Jericho's wall are very small. But many invisible barriers are equally as effective in keeping you out or hindering your progress in life and towards your desired goals. These invisible barriers can take many forms. Earlier, we saw how the practice of redlining is one of such barriers to wealth-building opportunities that people face in modern societies. Other barriers you may face today include prejudice, discrimination, lack of access to resources and opportunities, and financial and mental barriers such as self-doubt, fear, and limiting beliefs. All these can hinder you from reaching your full potential.

Like the Israelites had to overcome the physical barrier of the wall of Jericho, you also must tear down the invisible barriers that stand in your way; otherwise, you can be effectively shut out of what God has ordained for you. Thank God we have the story of the Wall of Jericho as an illustrative example of overcoming barriers in life.

How you can do this is the subject of the next section.

Breaking Through Limitations: By Faith

Today, the concept of a wall can take on various meanings and representations, often serving as a symbol of the challenges and obstacles we face. For some people, a wall can represent a hopeless situation where they feel trapped and unable to escape their circumstances. It can also mean a barrier that prevents them from reaching their goals or aspirations, leaving them feeling stuck and frustrated. Others may see a wall as a lack of progress, where they feel like they're not moving forward in life, or a dead end, where it feels like they've hit a point of no return.

Dead ends can be one of the most challenging barriers for people to recognize and overcome. Dead ends are situations or points in your journey where progress or forward movement becomes impossible or highly difficult. It describes a situation with no apparent solutions or opportunities for advancement. For example, people often face career dead ends, meaning that they feel stuck in their professional growth, lacking opportunities for advancement, or feeling unfulfilled in their current job. Dead ends can also be personal, in which case you feel lost, without direction, purpose, clarity, or motivation to move forward in your personal life. Many people also experience financial dead ends. When you hit a financial dead end, you face overwhelming debt, financial constraints, or an inability to improve your financial situation, leading to feeling trapped or stuck.

Regardless of the representation, a wall can be a daunting obstacle. It can leave you feeling discouraged, disheartened, and overwhelmed. However, it's important to remember that a wall is not an insurmountable barrier, and that the Bible has provided us with an example of overcoming it.

****

> "By faith, the walls of Jericho fell down after they were encircled for seven days."
> **Hebrews 11:30 NKJV**

Again, faith is the spiritual tool at our disposal for breaking down barriers in our lives. As such, there are certain faith principles that we can draw upon from the story of the Wall of Jericho.

Mental Barrier

One remarkable characteristic of the physical wall of Jericho was that it not only provided a physical barrier but also created a psychological one. Psychological barriers can create a mental block within you, impeding your progress and causing you to abandon your efforts.

When Moses first sent spies to survey Canaan, they returned with negative reports about the land. The spies commented that "the people who dwelt in the land are strong; the cities are fortified and very large; moreover, we saw the descendants of Anak there" (Numbers 14:28 NKJV). They saw the large, fortified cities and concluded that conquering the land and its inhabitants was impossible. The report discouraged the congregation. The physical wall that the spies saw already created a mental block to any possibility of their ability to conquer the land of Jericho. Through effective communication and imagery, they could transfer the same mental block to the entirety of the children of Israel, who, though they had not seen the physical wall, were convinced that they could do nothing to breach it. Some of the mental barriers you have in life are not the result of the actual things you have experienced or encountered, but they are stories of impossibilities that others have vividly described to you and have painted those images in your mind, preventing you from trying at all.

Most people don't know J.K. Rowling, but when you mention Harry Potter, it would be difficult to find a person who has not heard of Harry Potter. J.K. Rowling is the renowned author of the Harry Potter series. Before achieving massive success, Rowling faced numerous rejections from publishers for her first Harry Potter manuscript. As a result, her fear of failure became a significant barrier in her life.

Rowling was a single mother living on welfare then, and her financial struggles compounded her fear of failure. She battled self-doubt and uncertainty about her writing abilities and even questioned if she would ever find success as an author.

Despite facing numerous setbacks and rejections that were barriers to her, Rowling persevered. She refused to let the fear of failure hold her back and remained determined to bring her story to the world. Finally, in 1997, Bloomsbury Publishing took a chance on her manuscript, launching the phenomenon that would become the Harry Potter series.

Rowling's story is a testament to the power of perseverance in overcoming an invisible barrier. She could have allowed the rejections and self-doubt to paralyze her. Iinstead, she persisted and achieved unprecedented success as an author. Rowling's story is just one of a million examples of people facing barriers. But most people fail to overcome these barriers.

****

Visualization

Visualization is a process of creating mental images. It is a simple process whereby you picture what you want in and out of your life. You can use this technique to create a solid mental image of a future event. When dealing with barriers, visualization is a powerful tool that can replace images of failure with success, defeat with victory, and impossibilities with possibilities.

> The power of God's Word to change our lives lies in its ability to create images in our minds consistent with God's agenda.

Several years after the spies discouraged the hearts of the children of Israel by painting a picture of an impossibility to them, a new generation was getting ready to embark on the most crucial moment of their lives - entering their Promised Land. When they approached the city of Jericho, the first thing they saw was a giant, impregnable wall. However, the first thing they had to deal with was not the physical wall itself but the psychological effect of the wall coupled with the mental images they had of it through the stories they had heard for years.

To overcome this invisible barrier, God gave Joshua His Word as the primary tool.

> "And the LORD said to Joshua: 'See! I have given Jericho into your hand, its king, and the mighty men of valor'"
>
> **Joshua 6:2 NJKV**

The power of God's Word to change our lives lies in its ability to create images in our minds consistent with God's agenda. Without those images, we live in the default state of lack, fear, worry, anxiety, and timidity. God's first instruction to Joshua was to form a mental image of what He, the Lord, had already accomplished for them. While they saw a barrier wall, the Lord told Joshua, "See, I have given you Jericho." These words were promises of what God wanted to do for them and what He had already done. Using those words, they could form mental images of a defeated city rather than a wall-protected one. When God is about to do something in your life, He uses His Word to paint a picture of the desired state in your heart. You are responsible for taking those words and creating new images for your life.

Often, believers struggle because the world has painted images in people's minds that are inconsistent with the Word of God. Today, social media and mainstream media are aggressively competing for people's minds. The sad reality, however, is that these tools are constantly shaping the images of your mind. Again, because these things are battling for your attention, you barely have time to feed on the Word of God. As a result, they get free access into your mind, which then begins a cycle of determining your thought patterns and outlook. Now, it's time to get back into the Word of God. Let the Word of God be the primary agent that shapes your mind. Let God's Word paint images of possibilities in places where you think of impossibilities.

Today, social media and mainstream media are aggressively competing for people's minds. The sad reality, however, is that these tools are constantly shaping the images of your mind.

What images do you have in your mind? What are the invisible barriers in your path? To pull down those barriers, the pictures in your mind must first change to align with the reality you seek. Find scriptures that address whatever you are dealing with. Then, feed on God's Word until it creates a new image in your mind. To enter new realms and break barriers, you must first conceive it and see a new reality.

God's Way or No Way

As we discussed earlier, the walls of Jericho were a formidable obstacle built to withstand any external pressures.

Even with no known technology to breach it, the Israelites' faith in God allowed them to achieve the breakthrough they needed. This story teaches us that when faced with formidable barriers, your physical strength and energy alone may not be enough. Instead, you must rely on the power of God. Ultimately, you need faith to do the impossible. As the Lord said to Zerubbabel in Zechariah 4:6 NKJV, "Not by might nor by power, but by my Spirit." If your power cannot do it, it has to be done through the power of God and in His way. Even though you may struggle when God's way seems unreasonable, remember that 1 Corinthians 1:25 NKJV tells us, "The foolishness of God is wiser than men, and the weakness of God is stronger than men."

In the battle to breach the walls of Jericho, God had His way. Although it may have seemed strange at the time, God instructed the Israelites to march around the city once a day for six days without saying a word, with seven priests carrying trumpets made of rams' horns leading the way. On the seventh day, they were to march around the city seven times, and the priests would blow the trumpets, and all the people would shout with a great shout for the wall to fall.

There are a few faith principles that we can discuss from the above passage:

Breaking Through Limitations: Overcoming Systems and Structures

i. *Build your persuasion.*

The instruction to walk around the city of Jericho for six days without speaking was a test of faith for the Israelites. It required them to rely on God's power rather than their strength to overcome the barriers they faced. As they walked around the city, the soldiers of Jericho would have been watching and waiting for any sign of weakness or vulnerability.

During these six days, the Israelites would have had plenty of time to reflect on God's promise to give them the city. They would have had to trust in God's Word and believe He would fulfill His promise despite the seemingly impossible odds. Building such persuasion and conviction takes time, and the six days of walking around the city would have been a crucial period in strengthening the Israelites' faith. It required them to have patience and trust in God's timing as they waited for His plan to unfold. They would also have had to resist the temptation of not taking matters into their own hands. How many times would they have been tempted to try to breach the wall themselves?

> Feed on God's Word until it creates a new image in your mind.

Faith requires an absolute persuasion in God's promises. Building persuasion in the Word of God involves developing a strong belief and conviction in its truth and power. You are to believe it and be fully convinced and persuaded that it will happen exactly as God said it would. Romans 4:21 KJV says, "...and being fully persuaded that, what He had promised, He was able also to perform." Many people assume that they must only know what God promises. But there is the requirement of persuasion, just like Abraham. You must believe that God can do what He promised He would do. The Israelites couldn't do it themselves, so they had to be persuaded that God would do it.

Ultimately, the Israelites' obedience and faithfulness led to the miraculous defeat of Jericho. The lesson of this story is that you need to rely on God's power and timing, even when it doesn't make sense to you. You must trust in His promises and be patient while waiting for His plan to unfold.

To break down any wall or barrier in your life, you must build your persuasion that God can do what your strength alone cannot achieve for you.

Below are six steps to help you build a firm persuasion in God's promise:

1. Trust the Character of God: The Word of God is

rooted in God's exact nature and character. God is trustworthy, faithful, and true. Place your trust in Him and His Word, knowing He never fails to fulfill what He has spoken.

2. Study the Word: Take time to read and study the Bible regularly. Engage in deep reading, reflection, and meditation on the Scriptures. Studying the Word allows you to better understand God's promises, principles, and teachings.

3. Pray for Revelation: Ask God to reveal the depth and meaning of His Word to you. Pray for wisdom, understanding, and spiritual insight as you engage with Scripture. The Holy Spirit will illuminate the truth and give you a more profound revelation of God's Word.

4. Memorize Scripture: I know that scripture memorization is not widespread today, but committing key verses and passages to memory helps internalize God's Word. When you have Scripture stored in your heart, you can recall it in times of need, doubt, or uncertainty. Scriptural memorization also strengthens your confidence in the Word and its ability to guide and comfort you.

5. Meditate on God's Promises: Focus on specific promises and declarations in the Bible that relate to areas of your life where you desire persuasion. Reflect on God's faithfulness and track record of fulfilling His promises. Allow these promises to shape your thinking and build your trust in God's Word.

6. Apply the Word: Put the teaching and principles of the Bible into practice in your daily life. Observe how they bring about positive changes and transformation. As you experience the truth of God's Word firsthand, your confidence in its power grows.

ii. *God must go ahead of you.*

The instructions given to the Israelites before they marched around Jericho included carrying the Ark of the Covenant, a physical representation of God's presence. Carrying the Ark meant God's presence had to accompany them on their difficult task. As Isaiah 45:1-2 shows, God's presence goes before His people to make their crooked paths straight, subdue nations before them, and open doors that were once shut. The children of Israel needed this presence of God when they faced the seemingly impregnable walls of Jericho.

The presence of the Lord can help break down insurmountable barriers and obstacles. As God promised Cyrus in Isaiah 45:1-2, He will go before him, loosen the armor of kings, open doors, break the gates of bronze, and cut the iron bars. This same promise applies to believers today. When you face barriers, you need God's presence not only on your side but also to go ahead of you to prepare the way. By doing so, He can weaken the strength of those who stand against you and open the path to victory.

The presence of God is vital when you face difficulties and barriers. By following God's lead and trusting in His promises, you can rest assured that He will go before you, make your paths straight, and lead you to victory.

iii. *Believe it to see it.*

> "It shall come to pass, when they make a long blast with the ram's horn, and when you hear the sound of the trumpet, that all the people shall shout with a great shout, then the wall of the city will fall down flat."
>
> **Joshua 6: 5 NKJV**

Imagine walking around a giant impregnable wall for six days and, on the seventh day, having to do it seven times. Then, after the blast of a trumpet, you are supposed to shout and expect the wall of such a great magnitude to fall. That seems like a lot to ask for. Well, that is what faith is all about. You must first see it in the eyes of your mind and be persuaded that the power of God will accomplish it for you. Once these two ingredients are present, you don't have to see it physically before you shout triumphantly. Most people want to see the wall fall and then shout. But when you are operating in faith and trusting in God to accomplish things, you must first believe it before you can see it. For most people today, it is: "I will believe it when I see it," or "I will celebrate my victory when it happens," or "I will give my shouts when I see the walls come down." But the way of God is, if you want to see the wall come down, celebrate in advance, and then you will see it happen as God has told you.

When you believe in advance and celebrate in faith, you will see the manifestation of God's power as God told you. Again, the kind of faith that breaks down walls is based on the Word of God and not just mere wishful thinking. David said in Psalm 27:13 that I believed I would see God's goodness. He did not say; I would believe the goodness of God when I see. So, believe it to see it.

Faith Principles from This Chapter

2 Chronicles chapter 20 is about the story of Jehoshaphat, the King of Judah, who faced formidable opposition from a great multitude and their kings. Knowing that he could not win in his strength, Jehoshaphat sought the Lord, and

Breaking Through Limitations: Overcoming Systems and Structures

God sent a message through the prophet, Jahaziel.

God's message to Jehoshaphat was that he did not need to fear or be dismayed because the battle was not his but God's. God promised that the king of Judah and his people would not have to fight in the battle, but instead, they were to position themselves, stand still, and see the salvation of the Lord. Jehoshaphat rallied the people by admonishing them to believe in the Lord, their God, and trust His prophets.

Instead of waiting for the battle to begin, the people celebrated their victory in advance. They appointed those who would sing to the Lord and praise the beauty of His holiness. As they went out before the army, they sang praises to the Lord, saying, "Praise the LORD, for His mercy endures forever." As they sang, the Lord set ambushes against the enemy, and the Israelites defeated their enemies.

This passage highlights the same principles of faith seen in the story of Joshua and the walls of Jericho. The people received the Word of the Lord, became persuaded of His promises, and took the initiative to celebrate in advance of the victory. Ultimately, they did not have to fight because God fought for them, and their enemies turned against each other and destroyed each other. Therefore, let us learn from their example and trust in God's power, believe His promises, and celebrate our victory in advance through faith.

i. The Word of God preceded every action of faith. To act in faith is to have the Word of God backing every action.

ii. Be persuaded of God's promises that He will do exactly as He said.

iii. Believe to see.

iv. Celebrate as though what you are asking for is already done.

Here are some prayers and confessions to help you get started.

PRAYERS

1. Pray to God that He would reveal to you every known and unknown, invisible and visible, barrier you may be facing.

2. Pray that God will give you instructions on what to do to overcome every barrier in your life.

3. Pray that every man-made system that has been instituted or built to shut you out of your divine inheritances is brought down by the power of God.

CONFESSION

In the name of Jesus, every barrier in my path, either visible or invisible, is brought down by the power of God. I declare that God has gone ahead of me to level every mountain and every wall of barrier in my life. There are no more hindrances; I walk freely into my God-ordained life and destiny.

Reflective Questions

1. Can you identify the "walls" or obstacles in your path that require a similar faith-based approach to overcome?

2. Have you experienced moments in your life where faith played a significant role in dismantling barriers or obstacles? What did you learn from those experiences?

3. Are there barriers or walls in your life that you've held onto because they provide a sense of security, even if they limit your progress?

4. In what ways can you start taking practical steps today to apply the lessons of the story of the Wall of Jericho to your life and face your barriers with unwavering faith?

Faith in the Modern World

Action Note

Please use this section to write down things you will start doing based on what you have learned in this chapter.

CHAPTER 4

The Return of a Son

"The problem is not that we feel unworthy. The problem is that we believe it."

- **Unknown**

Have you ever been burdened by guilt from your past mistakes or overwhelmed by feelings of unworthiness in your relationship with God? Most people face this struggle in life. As a result, you can allow your experiences to define who you are. Because of your limited definition of self, you become content to settle for less than what you indeed are. In this chapter, we embark on a journey of how to uncover the profound influence of life experiences on your self-perception and identity. We'll explore how your setbacks and challenges can shape your identity, often leading you to settle for a diminished version of yourself. But fear not, for within these pages, we will discover how to reclaim your inherent worthiness and bask in the unyielding love and blessings God has destined for you. Join me as we unlock the transformative power of experiences and learn to embrace your true worth in the eyes of God.

The Departure into Desires

If you are familiar with Biblical stories, there is a good chance that you have heard or read about the Parable of the Prodigal Son. This Parable is one of the most famous parables of Jesus Christ. It is found in the Gospel of Luke 15:11-32 and tells the story of a father and his two sons. The younger son asks his father for his share of the inheritance, and the father agrees. The younger son then travels to a distant country and squanders his inheritance. When he has nothing left, he returns home to his father, expecting to be treated as a servant. However, his father is overjoyed to see him and welcomes him back with open arms. The father even throws a party in honor of his younger son and orders his servants to kill the fatted calf.

The older son then becomes angry when he sees what is happening, because he has been working hard for his father his entire life and feels as though he has been mistreated. As a result, he refuses to go to the party, and his father had to come out and plead with him. The older son eventually relents and joins the party but is still unhappy.

This Parable has been interpreted in many ways over the centuries. Some people see it as a story about the importance of repentance. In contrast, others see it as a story about the unconditional love of God. Regardless of how it is interpreted, the Parable of the Prodigal Son is a powerful and moving story that has resonated with people for centuries.

The focus of this chapter, though, will be on the prodigal son himself, how his experiences transformed his identity, and how he was able to reclaim that identity. Two aspects of this story are particularly interesting, and I would like you to journey with me in unraveling them. These two aspects are found in verses 18-19 of Luke chapter 15 NKJV. They are contained in this statement made by the prodigal son, "I will arise and go to my father, and will say to him, 'Father, I have sinned against heaven and before you, and I am no longer worthy to be called your son. Make me like one of your hired servants.'"

This chapter is titled "The Return of a Son." But we could say it is the return of a son coming back as an enslaved person.

No Longer Worthy!

Interestingly, it was after the prodigal son had wasted all of his inheritance that he came to a sudden realization to return to his father. And because of how he had lived in the past, he felt unworthy to be called a son. "And I am no longer worthy to be called your son…" Luke 15:19 NKJV.

Of all the explanations he could conjure up for his actions, the only one that made sense to him was the certainty that his prior actions had disqualified him from being a son. I wonder what happened to this prodigal son that moved him quickly from being a son who knew how to demand his rights from his father to a son who felt unworthy to be called a son and wanted to be treated like a slave. What we know is that he had some bitter experiences, and with those experiences, he lost his identity as a son.

Experiences don't leave people the same; in most cases, they contribute to a lasting sense of identity. The challenge is when your sense of identity is not rooted in the truth, and then you become defined by your life experiences. Your sense of identity affects how you think and how you ultimately act. Tony Robbins once said, "The strongest force in the whole human personality is this need to stay consistent with how we define ourselves." We all act consistently with who we believe we are. If you have the identity of a king, you'll always think and act like a king. In the same way, if you have the identity of an enslaved person, you'll consistently think and act like someone who is enslaved. Your thoughts and actions reflect your definition of who you are.

> We all act consistently with who we believe we are.

The Return of a Son

Bill Springfellow shared a powerful story in his 1984 book, *You Can Go Up*. The story goes that a group of barbers and stylists were looking for a way to showcase their work and show people how good they were at cutting hair, but they didn't know how to do it. So, they decided to hire a consultant, who told them they needed to get someone unkempt and give him a clean haircut. The consultant said that this would show people the difference between a good haircut and a bad haircut. The barbers and stylists were initially skeptical but decided to try it anyway. So, they found a homeless man who was very unkempt and gave him a clean haircut. The difference in his before and after pictures was drastic or mind-blowing. The homeless man looked utterly different after his haircut. He looked clean, well-groomed, and confident.

The barbers and stylists were so impressed with the results that they decided to use the homeless man as their poster child at their convention. They put his picture (before and after his transformation) on all their advertising and used him to show people how good they were at cutting hair.

On the day of the convention, they had three life-sized images of the man. The first was an image of him before the haircut, the second one after the haircut, and the third had him looking like an executive in a suit and tie. They also had a banner in the lobby that read, "See what the barbers and hairstylists of America can do to a man." The homeless man was in the lobby of the hotel, shaking people's hands and welcoming them to the convention.

The hotel manager was so impressed that he wanted to help the homeless man. He offered him a job and asked him to come the Monday after the convention. On Monday, the homeless man didn't show up as agreed. Some months later, the manager saw the three life-sized framed photos of the homeless man being used at the convention again. He grabbed one of them and ran downtown, asking people if they knew the man, but no one could identify him. Then the manager realized he had been using the frame of the man in suits. So, he ran back and took the first frame that had him the way he was initially. Within a short time, the manager located him. The homeless man was back to where he was before.

The lesson of this story is that the path to genuine and lasting transformation in individuals' lives commences with a shift in their self-perception or identity. What we believe about our identity is what we become. The barbers did a great job in transforming the homeless man from the outside. But this transformation didn't last because it did not affect his sense of identity; it was only an external change. True, lasting change must happen from the inside, starting from a change in the sense of identity.

> What we believe about our identity
> is what we become.

Like the homeless man, the prodigal son's experiences and everything that happened to him gradually stole away his identity as a son. And by the time he lost everything, nothing more in him made him feel worthy as a son. Suppose you have tied your identity to your right behaviors and moral conduct alone. In that case, it is inevitable that you'd feel unworthy to be called a son anytime you violate a moral code.

Consider the personality of this prodigal son for a moment. When first introduced to us, he is bold and knows his rights. So much so that he approached his father and demanded his inheritance even when the father was still alive. This bold move by the prodigal son is a definite indication that he is not a timid person at all. But once he allowed his experiences to shape the image of who he was, he adopted the identity that most adequately reflected his experience, the identity of a slave. Scriptures say the righteous are as bold as a lion. But even a lion loses his boldness when he stops thinking and seeing himself as a lion.

You may also be faced with the same dilemma. You are contemplating returning to God, or you have returned to God, but you feel inferior and totally unworthy to be called a child of God. Because of your past experiences, you feel this sense of guilt, judgment, and imminent condemnation hanging around your head. How can you fellowship with God when you feel unqualified every time you come to Him?

What have people said about you and to you, and what have your experiences taken away from your identity? You must consistently ask yourself: what identity are you currently adopting? Do you define yourself by how God identifies you, or have society, culture, and your own experiences shaped your identity?

Make Me Like a Hired Servant

The second aspect of the story of the prodigal son is in the second part of the statement he made in his contemplation of himself. He said, "And I am no longer worthy to be called your son, *make me like one of your hired servants.*" Luke 15:9 NKJV.

When your sense of identity in God becomes affected, you tend to develop limited expectations of what God can do for you. You can see yourself as undeserving of God's blessings and hesitate to ask for His provision, guidance, or intervention. This limited view of yourself can result in small, hesitant prayers that don't fully embrace the abundant promises and provisions that God offers.

Another way this lost sense of identity manifests is when you start to seek temporary fixes or quick solutions to your problems instead of addressing the underlying issues. You ask God for immediate relief rather than long-term holistic solutions. The prodigal son could have asked to be restored to his sonship position. Instead, he wanted to be like a hired servant.

The moment your identity is affected, you begin to disqualify yourself from the promises of God, the goodness of God, and your true inheritance in Him. You start to request from God things that are lesser than your true worth as a son/daughter of God. What would make a son start asking to become like a slave? The answer is what we have already looked at – identity. Because he lost his identity, the prodigal son was willing to become less of himself by asking to be made like one of the hired servants.

We have often preached about sinners returning to God, but how is the sinner returning to God? Are you in the kingdom taking your place, or as a slave who wants the crumbs from the kingdom?

The Identity of Righteousness

> "Don't count yourself out of God's promises; He had you in mind when He made them."

I once conversed with one of my cousins about the baptism of the Holy Spirit. I shared with him the story of how I got baptized in the Holy Spirit and my conviction that every believer needs to have the experience of the baptism of the Holy Spirit. From speaking with him, he strongly desired the experience as well. I told him it was easy and that once I prayed with him, he would get baptized in the Holy Spirit with the evidence of speaking in tongues. After praying with him, I noticed he had extreme resistance. When I asked why he strongly resisted, he responded, "I don't think I can ever get it." So, I asked him why he would say that, to which he gave me a shocking response. He said, "I have done so many horrible things in the past and feel that I am not qualified to get this gift." I asked him if he had confessed, prayed to God about them, and asked for forgiveness, and he said, "Yes." Then, I told him that God is not holding his past against him. I told him that once we confess our sins to God, He forgives us, but we are the ones who tend to hold on to those memories. To God, you are always His beloved child. Besides, I explained to him that God's gift to us is not a function of what we have done or haven't done in the past. God's gift is simply because of His generosity and who He is - a good God. As I spoke with him, I could see the sense of guilt and shame in him disappearing, and the more I talked, the more confident he became that he could receive the gift of the Holy Spirit. Of course, I prayed with him again. Before I finished praying, he was already praying out loud in his heavenly language - praise God.

So far in this book, we have been looking at the subject of faith and how we can apply faith principles in our modern world to overcome some of our contemporary challenges. Faith is a confident assurance that what we are expecting will happen. To have faith is to be convinced that God will do what He says He would do; it is a firm conviction that what you are believing for will be done. In other words, to have faith is to be confident. 1 John 5:14-15 NKJV says, "Now this is the confidence that we have in Him, that if we ask anything according to His will, He hears us. And if we know that He hears us, whatever we ask, we know that we have the petitions that we have asked of Him." However, you cannot have this kind of solid confidence in your dealings with God if you are harboring feelings of guilt, shame, or unworthiness.

I came across a powerful verse in Proverbs 2:21 NKJV, "For the upright will dwell in the land, and the blameless will remain in it." I quickly memorized this verse because I wanted to adopt it as one of my confessions. As I sat down meditating on the scripture, I started thinking that I did not qualify to use the verse because I wasn't sure I was blameless or upright. Then, the Holy Spirit spoke to my heart, and I will never forget it. He said, "Don't count yourself out of God's promises; He had you in mind when He made them." What causes the feeling of condemnation, guilt, shame, or unworthiness in your life, or in the life of any believer for that matter, is when you have lost your sense of righteousness. This is why the consciousness of righteousness is vital in your faith walk. To have and exercise strong faith, you must be righteousness-conscious.

What causes the feeling of condemnation,
guilt, shame, or unworthiness in your life,
or in the life of any believer for
that matter, is when you have lost your
sense of righteousness.

Righteousness has been defined as a right standing before God. The word "right standing" has a legal connotation. Think of someone who was tried before a legal system and received a favorable verdict of acceptability. With this verdict, he or she is declared right. Such a person is reported to be in good standing with society and in the eyes of the law. There are also some professional groups, alumni bodies, or other groups where your continued membership is based on your good standing with the committees. In this instance, good standing means that you have certified every requirement to have the rights and benefits of membership.

It is the same with righteousness. To be declared righteous is to have obtained the verdict of acceptability before God and certify all criteria and requirements to be declared right before God. It is what qualifies us to have the ability to stand before God. This knowledge enables you to stand before God, knowing that all requirements have been met and that you have the verdict of judgment in your favor.

Righteousness should be one of the primary identities of every believer. When you embrace righteousness, it becomes a defining characteristic of who you are and how you live your life. It shapes your values, choices, and behaviors. Righteousness allows you to stand boldly before God and have that firm conviction and confidence that what you are asking from God will be done. Righteousness gives you the consciousness to stand before God, having no sense of judgment, guilt, shame, condemnation, or unworthiness.

Therefore, most people ask, "How can these things be?" Or like Job asked, "Truly I know it is so, but how can a man be righteous before God?" Job 9:2 NKJV.

> Righteousness gives you the consciousness to stand before God, having no sense of judgment, guilt, shame, condemnation, or unworthiness.

You may also have these questions in your mind. Your past experiences and lifestyle may contribute to your feelings of inferiority and unworthiness with God. There is good news! God has made a way for men to be righteous before Him; that is what we will look at in the next session.

Becoming Righteous – By Faith

"By faith, Abel offered to God a more excellent sacrifice than Cain, through which he *obtained witness that he was righteous,* God testifying of his gifts; and through it he being dead still speaks." Hebrews 11:4.

Do you still remember Job's question, "How can a man be righteous before God?" The simple answer to that is?

You got it: by faith! However dark your past might be and however unqualified and unworthy you may be feeling today, you can still be made right with God, by faith.

In the scriptures, we find evidence that there are two ways in which righteousness is obtained. First is the righteousness that comes through the observance of the law. Second is the righteousness that is imputed by faith. Paul wrote in Philippians 3:9 NIV, "and be found in him, not having a righteousness of my own that comes from the law, but that which is through faith in Christ – the righteousness that comes from God on the basis of faith."

Outside In

The righteousness from the law is man's attempt to be made right with God through the observance of the law. Deuteronomy 6:24-25 NKJV reads, "And the LORD commanded us to observe all these statutes, to fear the LORD our God, for our good always, that He might preserve us alive, as it is this day. *Then it will be righteousness for us* if we are careful to observe all these commandments before the LORD our God, as He has commanded us." (Emphasis mine.) So, you see, the notion is when we observe the law, we will establish our own standard of righteousness for ourselves.

Many believers still hold this view on righteousness.

I call it the "outside-in" righteousness. Outside-in righteousness relies on external actions or appearances to establish one's righteousness. It suggests that one focuses on outward displays of righteousness without addressing the inner condition of the heart.

Reliance on external acts or rituals without addressing the internal state leads to superficiality. It becomes a matter of going through the motions or adhering to prescribed practices without genuine conviction or understanding of the underlying values and principles. One way to quickly identify this is when people project an image of righteousness to others while harboring conflicting thoughts, attitudes, or behaviors in private. This is so because the catalyst for personal growth and spiritual development is a genuine inner transformation. Relying solely on external acts or rituals without nurturing the inner self limits the potential for genuine character development. It also hinders the opportunity for self-reflection, self-awareness, and the cultivation of virtues and values that contribute to personal flourishing.

Some people still think the only way God can accept them is based on their morality and personal merit. This mindset gets people in trouble when it comes to receiving from God. Because, you see, once you think of your uprightness as the standard of God's righteousness, you will always find things in your life, your past, your character, and your conduct that would disqualify you.

Another limitation of the outside-in approach is that it tends to breed a kind of arrogance about your uprightness before God that sets you at odds with the grace of God. Through a thought-provoking parable, Jesus conveyed the impact of relying on self-righteousness as a hindrance to the grace of God.

> "To some who were confident of their own righteousness and looked down on everyone else, Jesus told this Parable: 'Two men went up to the temple to pray, one a Pharisee and the other a tax collector. The Pharisee stood by himself and prayed: 'God, I thank you that I am not like other people—robbers, evildoers, adulterers—or even like this tax collector. I fast twice a week and give a tenth of all I get.' 'But the tax collector stood at a distance. He would not even look up to heaven, but beat his breast and said, 'God, have mercy on me, a sinner.' "I tell you that this man, rather than the other, went home justified before God. For all those who exalt themselves will be humbled, and those who humble themselves will be exalted.'"
>
> **Luke 18:9-14 NIV**

Notice this person from the above passage and how he focused entirely on himself and the external things he did that made him feel qualified before God. But you see how the story ended? God justified the man who understood his state and asked for His help. Sadly, Israel had been focusing on this external means to attain righteousness. "But Israel, pursuing the law of righteousness, has not attained to the law of righteousness" Romans 9:31 NKJV. The simple reason for their failure is that righteousness cannot be attained by human efforts because "by the deeds of the law no flesh will be justified in the sight of God" – Romans 3:20 NKJV

So, righteousness by the standard of observing the law is only an illusion that is to be pursued but never attained and is never sufficient to measure up to the standards of God. By this measure, no man can be righteous before God. If you think what you do or don't do is what would determine your righteousness before God, then you have automatically disqualified yourself by default. Galatians 5:4 NLT reminds us, "For if you are trying to make yourselves right with God by keeping the law, you have been cut off from Christ! You have fallen away from God's grace." By nature, we, as humans, cannot measure up to God's standard of righteousness. Any attempt to work for it always results in misery and futility. "For they don't understand

God's way of making people right with himself. Refusing to accept God's way, they cling to their own way of getting right with God by trying to keep the law. For Christ has already accomplished the purpose for which the law was given. As a result, all who believe in him are made right with God." Romans 10:3 & 4 (NLT)

> So, righteousness by the standard of observing the law is only an illusion that is to be pursued but never attained and is never sufficient to measure up to the standards of God. By this measure, no man can be righteous before God.

Inside Out

However, another kind of righteousness is spoken of in the Bible: the righteousness of faith. This righteousness is the righteousness of God Himself. Paul wrote that the Gospel is a revelation of the righteousness of God (Romans 1: 16-17 NKJV.) We find another reference of the righteousness of God in Romans chapter 3, "But now the righteousness of God apart from the law is revealed, being witnessed by the Law and the Prophets, even the righteousness of God through faith in Jesus Christ, to all and on all who believe. For there is no difference." Romans 3: 21-22 NKJV

Since man cannot attain the standard of God's righteousness through mere observance of the law, God found a way to declare man righteous, and that can only be accomplished through faith in Christ Jesus.

This kind of righteousness is what I call inside-out righteousness. It originates from a genuine inner transformation and reflects outwardly in one's thoughts, attitudes, and actions. This kind of righteousness focuses on the human heart, which then influences and guides behavior consistently and authentically.

Inside-out righteousness is not dependent on your conduct or past actions and inactions. Instead, it is a righteousness that is imputed. In other words, it is a gift God bestows on His children for having faith in Him. Like Abraham, the scriptures say, he "believed God, and it was accounted to him for righteousness." (Romans 4:3 NKJV). This type of declarative righteousness from God is not only for Abraham. In other words, the example of faith that leads to righteousness before God was not written for Abraham's sake alone, "But also, for us. It shall be imputed to us who believe in Him who raised up Jesus our Lord from the dead." Romans 4:24 NKJV. The purpose of the example of Abraham is to show how Abraham's faith brought about his righteousness and how the same can happen to us.

By far, righteousness by faith is simpler than trying to gain righteousness by your deeds and conduct, which is impossible. And how does this righteousness by faith happen? You believe in Jesus Christ, that He died as your substitute, and put your trust in Him. Once you do this, this gift of righteousness is part of your welcome package into God's family. God made Jesus, who knew no sin, to be sin for us, that we might become the righteousness of God in Him. (2 Corinthians 5:17). The moment you dedicated your life to God through faith in Christ Jesus was the moment God clothed you in His righteousness.

The Full Assurance of Faith

When your sense of identity is rooted internally, not in what you have done but in what God, through Christ, has done for you, then you will be better equipped to navigate challenges and temptations. The strength of inner convictions provides you with a solid foundation during times of moral dilemmas, external pressures, or societal influences that may contradict your values.

Let's briefly revisit the story of the prodigal son. After his speech of repentance to his father, that is, being unworthy to be called a son and, as a result, wanting to be made like a servant, his father responded with an unexpected gesture. "But the father said to his servants, 'bring out the best robe and put it on him, and put a ring on his hand, and sandals on his feet.'" Luke 15:22 NKJV. This father deeply understood that his son had lost his identity of being a son. Therefore, the first thing he did was dress his son with all the symbols representing him in his identity as a son. The prodigal son was then restored to his right standing with his father.

To have the confidence of right fellowship with God, you must first be dressed in your complete identity as His child. That is what God's righteousness does for you. It gives you a sense of worthiness, not because of what you have done, for if by that only, you deserve judgment, but by the measure of the love of the Father, which has restored you to the right standing with Him. The righteousness of faith qualifies you, not based on your performance, but on Christ's performance.

Faith requires an understanding that there is nothing that disqualifies you. Because if you feel disqualified, you cannot have the confidence necessary to go before God.

That is why the prodigal son's father had to dress him like a son first before he allowed his son to even speak to him. Before you go to God, make sure your identity in Him is rooted in your righteousness in Christ.

With this new consciousness of your righteousness, you can approach God with boldness and claim what He has for you by faith because you know that there is no more condemnation, guilt, and shame.

Romans 8:34 NKJV says, "Who is he who condemns? It is Christ who died, and furthermore is also risen, who is even at the right hand of God, who also makes intercession for us." And because of what Christ did, "there is therefore now no condemnation to those who are in Christ Jesus, who do not walk according to the flesh, but according to the Spirit." Romans 8:1 NKJV. So there is no more condemnation because God declared you righteous. And since there is no more condemnation and shame, we can have the boldness to enter into the presence of God as there is a new way that has been set apart for this purpose.

Sometimes, I hear Christians pray and say, "I am not worthy to come before you." And when they pray like this, they sound so spiritual. I understand if you say that by yourself you are not worthy, but you see, you are no more of yourselves. You are now in Christ. His righteousness is your righteousness. That is why Scripture says, "Let us therefore come boldly to the throne of grace, that we may obtain mercy and find grace to help in time of need." Hebrews 4:16 NKJV.

PRAYERS

1. Pray that God will open the eyes of your understanding to see how much He loves you.

2. Pray for more revelation of your identity in Christ and how faith in Christ Jesus has made you righteous in Him.

3. Pray that the Blood of Jesus will cleanse you from every sin and every form of unrighteousness.

4. Pray that every consciousness of guilt, condemnation, and shame for actions in the past be erased by the Blood of Christ

CONFESSION

I declare that by faith in Christ Jesus, I am made righteous. God has qualified me in His love, and therefore nothing disqualifies me. Every handwriting of requirement written against me has been nailed to the cross. I am free from shame, guilt, and condemnation in Jesus' mighty name.

Reflective Questions

1. Can you identify practical steps or changes in mindset that will help you more consistently live in your righteous identity as a child of God?

2. Are there specific beliefs or self-criticisms that you need to release to fully embrace your righteous identity in Christ?

3. Can you recall moments in your life when you felt distant from God, akin to the prodigal son's separation from his father? What helped you find your way back?

4. In what ways have you sought to establish your identity or worth through personal achievements and works, only to find that it fell short of true fulfillment?

Action Note

Please use this section to write down things you will start doing based on what you have learned in this chapter.

CHAPTER 5

And He Went Out, Not Knowing Where He Was Going

> "In the adventure of faith, the destination may be unknown, but the Guide is always trustworthy."
>
> **- Lysa Terkeurst.**

In 2015, while in Nigeria, I strongly desired to pursue my master's degree in the United States. With limited means and resources, I only knew that I needed a master's degree, and the U.S. was the ideal destination. However, I also sensed the Lord prompting me to attend a Bible school during this period. Initially, I couldn't comprehend the connection between Bible school and a master's degree, and Bible school at the time seemed unrelated to all my career plans. Don't get me wrong, I had a strong desire to deepen my knowledge and love for God, but I did not comprehend the necessity of Bible school since I felt Bible school is for those who are considering active ministry.

Nevertheless, I reluctantly obeyed and enrolled in Bible school, thinking I would complete my first year and then proceed with my plans to pursue a master's degree. Little did I know it, but God had a different plan. I faced many challenges in finalizing the process for my desired school in the U.S., which left me devastated. God continued nudging me to enroll in the second year and complete the Bible school program. Once again, I hesitantly followed His lead.

An unexpected turn of events unfolded during my second year of Bible school. The process for my travel to the United States started falling into place. I began making arrangements for the move despite having no resources or connections in the U.S. In fact, at that point, I didn't know anyone residing in the U.S. However, while at Bible school, I encountered a pastor who would play a significant role in assisting me upon my arrival in the United States. Through his connections, I found a place to stay. I was introduced to opportunities that would later play a huge part in completing my program.

Looking back, I realize I did not understand God's ultimate plan when this journey began. Each decision and direction He led me in seemed puzzling at the time. However, in retrospect, all the pieces fit together perfectly. I now understand why God wanted me to take specific steps before moving forward. His guidance was purposeful and strategic, even when I couldn't see the bigger picture. Philip Yancey once said, "Faith means believing in advance what will only make sense in reverse."

In summary, the process I underwent had its challenges and uncertainties. Yet, as I obediently followed God's leading, doors opened, connections were made, and provisions came forth. It is now evident that God's plan for me was far greater than I initially envisioned. Through the detour of Bible school, I gained sound biblical and doctrinal knowledge. I cultivated a stronger faith and a clearer sense of purpose.

> "Faith means believing in advance what will only make sense in reverse."
> — Philip Yancey

As I reflect upon my journey, I am reminded of the countless stories in the Bible where individuals were called to venture into the unknown, relying solely on their faith in God's guidance. From Abraham leaving his homeland to Moses leading the Israelites through the wilderness, and from David facing Goliath to the disciples forsaking everything to follow Jesus, the common thread woven through these narratives is the unwavering trust placed in God's leading, even when the destination remained shrouded in mystery.

In a world that often celebrates meticulous planning, calculated risks, and clearly defined pathways, surrendering control and embracing the unknown can be daunting. Yet, it is within these uncharted territories that our faith is being tested and refined and that is where our most significant spiritual growth occurs.

Beyond Logic and Reason

As human beings, we are creatures of habit and we like to know what to expect. We find security in the predictable routines and environment we've grown accustomed to. The unknown is full of unanswered questions and potential risks. Therefore, deciding to leave the familiarity of the known and step into the uncertainty of the unknown is challenging; it requires courage, resilience, and a willingness to embrace change and growth.

The big question, therefore, is, what is the essential ingredient I need to summon the courage to leave behind the security of my present circumstances and dive into the vast unknown, where untapped potential and extraordinary possibilities await? How can I overcome the fear of uncertainty and embrace the journey of exploration? The answer, my friend, lies in just these two words: by faith. Faith is the key to embarking on a transformative journey into the unknown, where you can discover new opportunities

And He Went Out, Not Knowing Where He Was Going

and personal growth.

****

In today's fast-paced and ever-changing world, people face various decisions when venturing into the unknown. Here are a few examples:

Career Changes: many individuals find themselves at a crossroads in their professional lives, contemplating whether to leave the stability of their current job or industry to pursue a new path. This decision involves stepping into unfamiliar territory, exploring new sectors, acquiring new skills, and taking calculated risks to unlock greater career fulfillment.

Entrepreneurship: Starting a business is an exciting yet uncertain endeavor. It requires individuals to leave the security of a regular paycheck and embrace the challenges of building something from scratch. Entrepreneurs must navigate uncharted waters, face financial risks, and trust in their vision and abilities to create a successful venture.

Relocation: Moving to a new city or country often involves entering the unknown. It requires individuals to leave behind their familiar surroundings, support systems, and established routines. Relocating also entails adapting to a different culture, establishing new connections, and embracing the opportunities and challenges that come with a fresh start.

Personal Relationships: Taking the leap into a new romantic relationship or committing to a significant change in an existing one can be a journey into the unknown. It involves opening oneself up to vulnerability, trusting in the relationship's potential, and embracing the uncertainties that come with deep emotional connections.

Personal Growth and Self-Discovery: Embarking on a journey of personal growth often requires individuals to step out of their comfort zones and explore new experiences. New experiences may involve:

- Traveling alone.
- Trying new hobbies or interests.
- Pushing past fears and limitations.
- Embracing opportunities for self-discovery and self-improvement.

These are just a few examples of the decisions people face when considering venturing into the unknown. Each decision presents unique challenges and rewards, requiring individuals to summon courage, embrace uncertainty, and trust the journey ahead.

Sometimes, It's Okay Not to Know

I remember the pressure I felt upon completing a master's degree program in 2019. Everyone seemed interested in asking, "So, what is next?" or "What do you plan on doing next?" Trust me, this question is much more challenging to answer than it appears. Having just completed a degree and invested time and money in studying, there was an expectation from society that I had all the details of my life figured out. This societal expectation adds additional pressure to be well-informed and knowledgeable.

Asking people questions like "What is next?" fits into our modern society's undeniable obsession with knowledge and the quest to figure everything out. Today's culture highly values information and emphasizes knowing every detail and how things fit together. For instance, before we go out to eat at a restaurant, my wife extensively researches all there is to know about it. She enjoys gathering information about the food they offer, the restaurant's environment, the distance to get there, and even the parking availability. Online reviews provide further insights into people's experiences. We do this to ensure we have as much information as possible before stepping out into an unfamiliar place and deciding where to eat. We want to avoid going to a place where we don't know what to expect.

One reason for this obsession with knowing is the technological advancement which has made vast amounts of information easily accessible. We can delve into an endless sea of knowledge with just a few clicks. This convenience and speed of information retrieval has fueled our desire to know more. We are constantly bombarded with new information through social media, news outlets, and search engines. This constant consumption of knowledge leads us to believe that the more we know, the better equipped we are to make well-informed choices. However, that is not always the case.

Consider the approach of Bobby Fischer, one of the greatest chess players ever. Fischer's rise to fame came in the late 1950s and early 1960s when he won several U.S. Chess championships and represented the United States in international competitions. Fischer's playing style was known for its strategic brilliance and uncompromising approach. He deeply understood the game and was exceptionally skilled at positional play. Fischer's attention to detail and ability to calculate moves set him apart from his opponents.

In the 2014 biographical drama *Pawn Sacrifice*, directed by Edward Zwick and starring Tobey Maguire as chess prodigy Bobby Fischer, Fischer's rise to fame as a chess champion and highly publicized 1972 World Chess Championship match against Soviet grandmaster Boris Spassky during the Cold War are carefully portrayed. Game 6 of the championship match was considered by many to be the greatest chess game ever played. After the game, Fischer's trainer commented on his chess skills, saying, "The chess you've been playing is really inspired." Fischer's response was, "It's almost all theory and memorization. People think there are all these options, but there's usually one right move."

This statement highlights an essential aspect of Bobby Fischer's approach to chess: his exceptional ability to focus on the immediate move rather than getting overwhelmed by considering multiple moves ahead. While some chess players strategize by thinking several moves forward and analyzing various possibilities, Fischer believes in the power of making the best move in the present moment.

When you desire to walk with God, it is essential to give up the need to know every specific detail of His plans. You must be comfortable with not knowing sometimes and trust Him to reveal each step of His plan. A proper walk with God is a walk of faith; remember, "For we walk by faith and not by sight." 2 Corinthians 5:7 NKJV

Like Bobby Fischer, you must learn to take it one move

at a time. It is okay not to have all the detailed plans when venturing into the unknown. Not having everything figured out will teach you to rely on God to show you each move along the way, allowing Him to direct you into His plan step by step. Understand that you will not figure everything out. God deliberately withholds certain information from you because the journey He takes you on requires faith.

****

Throughout this book, we have examined how faith is the underlying variable that allows people to accomplish great things that seem to be beyond human possibilities. Let's consider another example of Abraham and how he could follow God into the unknown by faith.

"By faith Abraham obeyed when he was called to go out to the place which he would receive as an inheritance. And he went out, not knowing where he was going." Hebrews 11:8 NKJV

Abraham is our prototype of someone who dared to leave his familiar territory and embark on a journey he knew nothing about. Let's take a deeper dive into his story and see what enabled him to make such a decision and what guaranteed his success.

And He Went Out, Not Knowing Where He Was Going

The story starts in Genesis chapter 12:1 NKJV, "Now the LORD had said to Abram: 'Get out of your country, from your family, and from your father's house to a land that I will show you.'"

From this verse of scripture, I have identified four things that happened in the story of Abraham that enabled him to have a successful experience when he ventured into the unknown. These are:

- He heard from God.
- He was willing to leave his comfort zone.
- He believed where God was taking him was better.
- Abraham obeyed and acted.

Hear from God

Abraham's journey into uncharted territories started with "Now the LORD had said." Many people assume that faith means taking risks when the outcomes are unknown. No, that is not faith. Walking by faith is rooted in an unshakable trust and belief in God's Word. Taking risks, on the other hand, is more focused on evaluating potential gains and losses, weighing probabilities, and making calculated decisions based on personal judgment. Therefore, one can say that taking risks is based on human calculation. Faith, however, relies on divine instructions.

I often hear one statement today: "I took the leap of faith." When people say this, what they invariably mean is they made a decision when they weren't sure of the outcome. But faith is to be certain of an outcome yet to happen; that certainty is based on the Word of God.

Faith is taking action because "God said." But unfortunately, what some people call faith is their insistence on a particular outcome. When people say they are standing in faith, we should ask, "Based on what?" What are you standing on? You cannot insist on what you want to happen; that is presumption, not faith.

My advice to people, especially when making life-altering decisions like relocation, marital choices, and career decisions, is always to "make sure God is leading you." You can avoid making many wrong choices if you wait patiently to hear from God before acting.

In Nigeria, a recent trend called "JAPA" has gained prominence. It refers to the act of relocating to another country in search of a better life. This trend has witnessed many individuals making concerted efforts to leave Nigeria behind and pursue opportunities abroad. However, this has sparked a response from prominent figures within the country, some of whom have spoken out against the trend. Certain voices, particularly those from religious perspectives, have encouraged people to remain in Nigeria instead of opting for "Japa."

In addition, some individuals have actively encouraged young people to take every possible step to "Japa." However, when it comes to this matter, my perspective is straightforward: ensure that you are seeking God's guidance before making any decisions. Whether you stay in your current location or pursue a new one, the crucial factor is aligning with God's will for your life at any moment. It is essential not to leave if God intends for you to stay and not to stay if God intends for you to go.

Hebrews 11:29 AMPC says, "[urged on] by faith the people crossed the Red Sea as [though] on dry land, but when the Egyptians tried to do the same thing they were swallowed up [by the sea]." This scripture shows two groups of people making the same movement but experiencing different outcomes. What guarantees a successful outcome is faith that is prompted by the Word of God. When the Word of God precedes your actions, you will attempt things that seem naturally impossible. And when others who do not have the same instruction attempt to imitate your actions, they get drowned. Many people find themselves in situations and circumstances that would have been avoidable if they had waited patiently to hear from God. Remember, "the Lord said" is the difference between taking risks and taking steps of faith.

Give Up Your Comfort Zone

The unknown can be intimidating and unpredictable. For this reason, people naturally seek stability and security, and stepping into the unknown challenges those desires. Fear of the unfamiliar and the potential risks and consequences can lead individuals to avoid making decisions that would take them into uncharted territory. Generally, humans tend to prefer what is familiar and comfortable. Stepping into the unknown means venturing outside one's comfort zone, which can be uncomfortable and unsettling. Many people prefer to stay within the boundaries of what they already know and are accustomed to, even if it means missing out on potential growth and opportunities.

God told Abram, "Get out of your country, from your family, and your father's house." In the context of this instruction, "country," "family," and "father's house" can be seen as symbolic representations of the various attachments and sources of security that individuals often have in their lives.

Country: The "country" represents Abram's geographical location, homeland, and cultural and societal norms. It signifies a place where he has a sense of belonging, familiarity, and identity. Leaving his country indicates detachment from the comfort and security of staying within the confines of what is known and predictable.

Family: The "family" represents Abram's immediate relatives, including his parents, siblings, and extended family. Family ties often provide a strong sense of support, identity, and stability. By asking Abram to leave his family, God calls him to detach from the close relationships and emotional ties that can hinder his complete obedience and reliance on God's guidance.

Father's House: The "father's house" refers to Abram's ancestral home, where he grew up, and his family heritage. It represents the traditions, values, and legacy that have shaped him. Leaving his father's house signifies a departure from the generational influences and patterns that may have defined his life up to that point. It involves breaking away from the expectations and limitations imposed by his lineage and stepping into a new future.

How attached are you to your comfort zone? Attachments can hinder your willingness to embrace the unknown and follow God's leading. Following God's plan requires you to let go of attachments and place your trust entirely in God's plan, purpose, and guidance.

The Promise of Something Better

Something hilarious happened to me back in August 2017. I had only been in the U.S. for a mere five days! On this occasion, I attended the orientation organized for graduate students at the school I would be attending. After the orientation, out of the blue, this guy strolled up to me and introduced himself. We exchanged names and where we were from, and then he dropped the bombshell. He asked if I'd accompany him to grab a check from some mysterious place. I couldn't believe it. I looked at him from head to toe, thinking, "Are you out of your mind? I barely know you, and you want me to embark on an adventure to an unknown destination with you?" Maybe it'd be a different story if I were more familiar with the area, but I had only been on the campus twice. I hadn't yet mastered the art of finding my way from home to school! Can you believe it?

If you are curious about how it ended, here it is. I reluctantly agreed to follow this unknown fellow to an unknown location. While we were walking, I couldn't get it out of my mind that this could be the start of a horror movie. I bet I wasn't listening to anything he said while we were on the way. I was hoping I would get back to the campus in one piece. Thankfully, nothing happened. We got to the place, he picked up the check, and we returned to the campus. As it turns out, that would be the start of many unplanned adventures with him because we became very good friends after that day.

When God told Abraham, "Get out of your country, from your family, and from your father's house *to a land that I will show you,"* perhaps, because of my own experience, I can imagine a conversation in this manner:

God: "Leave everything behind and come with me."

Abraham: "Where exactly are we going?"

God: "Come with me, and I will show you."

Abraham "Ummmm, creepy! You can't even tell me where we are going, and you want me to leave all the good things I have around here?"

God: "Yes, that's exactly what I am saying. I will make it worthwhile for you, though."

Abraham: "Okay, lead the way."

Decisions about the unknown can be challenging, with limited information or uncertainty about potential outcomes. People may hesitate to take action without clearly understanding the risks and rewards. They may prefer to gather more information or wait for a clearer picture before deciding.

We can now understand Abraham's complete trust in God, in that He was willing to follow God's leading, even without knowing the specific details or location of the land beforehand.

This type of willingness to follow without knowing about the specifics requires trust. And that trust can only come from a deep conviction that the other person has your best interests at heart. It is best built on familiarity and understanding. When we don't know someone well, we lack the necessary information and experiences to assess their character, intentions, and reliability. Many still struggle to believe God has their best interests at heart. You may know and believe that God is good, but do you believe that God is good to you? Do you believe He has your best interests at heart and will do everything in His power to make you successful? Suppose you struggle with acknowledging and accepting the goodness of God. In that case, you will struggle to follow Him when He guides you into the unknown. Proverbs 3:5 & 7 CEV says, "With all your heart you must trust the Lord and not your own judgment. Always let him lead you, and he will clear the road for you to follow."

Another reason Abraham could follow God was because he had the promise of something better. When God called him into the unknown, God also promised what would happen when he agreed to go on this journey.

"I will make you a great nation; I will bless you and make your name great; and you shall be a blessing. I will bless those who bless you, and I will curse him who curses you; and in you all the families of the earth shall be blessed." Genesis 12:2-3 NKJV

God has preordained each of us to fit perfectly into the purpose of His will. God's plan for your life precedes whatever plan you may have. And His plan is way better and supersedes whatever you can develop. He has a plan for your life, and He has a plan for your future. In His divine wisdom, He has also designed the best pathways to get you to the destination He has in mind. That is why you must trust Him. You can claim the good life that He has prearranged for you only when you follow the pathways He has prepared and do the good works that he has planned for you.

Take Action

There is this saying that "The journey of a thousand miles starts with a single step." I like to have all the information I need before committing to the first step. But I have observed that nothing in life cripples you more than this. So, I am learning to take it one step at a time. I don't have to see how all the pieces fit with one another; I need to focus on taking the first step.

That is why I like how the story of Abraham unfolds. Genesis 12:4 NKJV says, "So Abram departed as the LORD had spoken to him, and Lot went with him. And Abram was seventy-five years old when he departed from Haran."

First, you see how it says, "Abram departed," not arrived. The moment he decided to take action was not when he arrives precisely where God wanted him to be, but the process had to start with him taking the first step.

Once we act on the Word of God, He takes responsibility for guiding us to our destination. He says, "I will guide you along the best pathway for your life. I will advise you and watch over you." Psalms 32:8 NLT. God has given you His promise to guide you. But that promise depends on your taking action. You cannot expect God's guidance along the best pathways when you are unwilling to commit to the first step.

PRAYERS

1. Pray that God will give you the grace to follow Him wherever He calls you, even into the unknown.

2. Pray that you will be spiritually attuned to hear whenever God calls upon you.

3. Pray that, like Abraham, you will obey God even when you cannot reason out His directions.

CONFESSION

The Lord is instructing and leading me in the ways that I should go. His loving eyes are guiding me. My spirit is alive and sensitive to the leading of the Lord, and I have a willing heart to go in the direction that God is leading me even when it does not make sense to me.

Reflective Questions

1. What are the parallels between Abraham's willingness to follow God and the concept of stepping out in faith in your own faith journey?

2. Can you identify specific decisions or actions in your life that required you to trust God's guidance even when the path was unclear? How did those experiences shape your faith?

3. In what ways has stepping into the unknown and

embracing uncertainty been a catalyst for personal growth, spiritual development, or unexpected blessings in your life?

4. Can you relate to moments in your own life when you followed a path without a clear destination in sight? What emotions and challenges did you experience during such times?

5. Reflect on a time when you felt a strong calling or leading, similar to Abraham's experience. How did you discern this calling, and what motivated you to follow it?

And He Went Out, Not Knowing Where He Was Going

Action Note

Please use this section to write down things you will start doing based on what you have learned in this chapter.

CHAPTER 6

Frame Your World

"The universe is a masterpiece of awe-inspiring elegance, with its celestial bodies shining brightly, painting the canvas of the cosmos with dazzling colors and patterns."

– Unknown.

The universe we inhabit is mind-bogglingly immense and wondrous. It is an intricately woven tapestry where celestial bodies dance in perfect harmony, shaping the conditions necessary for life to flourish. From galaxies to stars, the sun, the moon, and everything in between, each element plays a crucial role in creating the habitable environment we call home. Every cosmic detail plays its part in the symphony of life.

Everything in the universe must be held in perfect harmony. For instance, if the sun were significantly closer to the Earth, the increased radiation and heat would have severe consequences. It could also lead to extreme temperatures, making life challenging to survive. If the sun were much farther away, the Earth would receive insufficient sunlight and heat, resulting in extremely cold conditions that would also make it difficult for life to thrive, which means that the sun had to be at a precise distance from the Earth for the planet to be habitable.

For years, understanding the universe has been the pursuit that engages astronomers, physicists, cosmologists, and other scientific disciplines. Human knowledge of the universe continues to expand. Yet people involved in these disciplines maintain that many mysteries remain, such as the nature of dark matter and dark energy, the origins of the universe, and the possibility of extraterrestrial life.

That is why, in our world today, space exploration is a hot topic that is generating significant interest and discussion across various fields. It continues to inspire awe and push the boundaries of human knowledge. It holds the potential for profound discoveries and advancement that can benefit humanity and deepen our understanding of the universe we inhabit. Future space exploration goals include:

- Returning humans to the moon through programs like NASA's Artemis mission.
- Crewed missions to Mars.
- Establishing permanent human settlements in space.

Private companies, such as SpaceX and Blue Origin,

play an increasing role in space exploration and commercial space travel.

How did everything come together in perfect harmony?

The God Kind of Faith

> "By faith we understand that the entire universe
> was formed at God's command, that what we
> now see did not come from anything
> that can be seen."
>
> **Hebrews 11:3 NLT**

In Mark Chapter 11, Jesus and His disciples were going to Jerusalem from Bethany. Then they saw a fig tree, and Jesus wanted to eat the figs because He was hungry. On getting close to the tree, He found that there was no fruit, only leaves on the tree. Then He said, "Let no one eat fruit from you ever again." The following day, to the utter amazement of the disciples, they saw the fig tree dried to the roots. Jesus, in response, answered them, "Have faith in God." If you read the margins from your Bible, you'd see that the original translation of this statement means "have the God kind of faith." You may be wondering, what exactly is God's kind of faith? I believe the disciples also wanted to know what it meant to have the God kind of faith. Jesus, not intending to leave His disciples in confusion about what He meant, explained God's kind of faith. He said, "For assuredly, I say to you, whoever says to this mountain, 'Be removed and be cast into the sea,' and does not doubt in his heart, but believes that those things he says will be done, he will have whatever he says." Mark 11:23 NJKV

Here, you see that God kind of faith operates by speaking. To operate the God kind of faith, two things are necessary. First, you must say what you want to happen. Second, you must believe, without doubt, that the things you say will come to pass. This is the God kind of faith: believe it, then speak it.

So, when Jesus said to "have faith in God," He meant, like God, to speak into existence the things you want to happen in your world. Right from the beginning, God's primary tool of creation is His Word. "All things were made through Him [the Word], and without Him [the Word] nothing was made that was made." (John 1:3 NKJV)

When you look at creation today and the universe, you see the beauty of creation, how intricately woven everything is, and how everything operates in perfect harmony. But how did God bring about the astounding beauty that is the universe? We know that in the beginning, God created the heavens and the Earth, and there was chaos and

Frame Your World

disorder until God started speaking. Look at the verses below and see the common theme in everything God created; they were preceded by what He said.

Genesis 1:3, "Then God said…"

Genesis 1:6, "Then God said…"

Genesis 1:9, "Then God said…"

Genesis 1:11, "Then God said…"

Genesis 1:14, "Then God said…"

Genesis 1:20, "Then God said…"

Genesis 1:24, "Then God said…"

Genesis 1:26, "Then God said…"

God spoke into existence everything He wanted in creation. And when He was done speaking, Genesis 1:31 says, "Then God saw…" That is God's kind of faith; He spoke things into existence and saw everything He had spoken come to pass. Hebrews 11:3 can be paraphrased as, "We understand that by faith, God framed the worlds so that the things we can physically see were not made from physical materials, but by the words of God."

God not only created the world by His words, but even the sustenance of the entire world is hanging on the integrity of the Word of God.

The Same Spirit of Faith

We have seen that God's kind of faith speaks nonexistent things into physical realities. One of the "Then God said" statements was about the creation of man (human being) himself. After this statement follows: "So God created man in His own image; in the image of God, He created him; male and female He created them." Of all God's creation, only man was created in the image of God. Being made in the image of God suggests that human beings share some inherent qualities or attributes of God. One such is the capacity for speech. With humans' ability for speech, it means, like God, they can order their world through speech.

You have discovered true power when you realize that your words spoken in faith can transform your life.

If words are the primary tool God used in creating the known world, you, made in His image, can also create your world with your words. Until this point in your life, *your words have been the active, creative agents in shaping your realities; you may not be aware of it. Also Your words are active, creative agents that will shape your future realities.*

Operating in the spirit of faith means that you are aware that the power of your words can change your reality, and you are consciously using your words to that effect. You have discovered true power when you realize that your words spoken in faith can transform your life. Paul wrote, "And since we have the same spirit of faith, according to what is written, 'I believed and therefore I spoke,'" we also believe and therefore speak.'" 2 Corinthians 4:13 NKJV. In this scripture, Apostle Paul was quoting what David said in Psalms that he believed and therefore he spoke. He says the spirit of faith has two components: believing and speaking.

You can have faith in your heart, but you can only release the faith when you speak it. Although it is true that faith is of the heart or comes from the heart, it can only be released with the mouth. Faith in the heart that is not released through the mouth is like a loaded gun without a trigger. However loaded a gun is, its potency is only felt when the trigger is released. Remember, you are created in the image of God, and we have seen how God's faith operates. God didn't only imagine the world He wanted to make; He also had to speak it into existence.

Faith in the heart that is not released through the mouth is like a loaded gun without a trigger.

Customize Your World

> "The best way to predict the future
> is to create it."
>
> **- Peter Drucker**

My wife and I took a car for a test drive. At the time, we chose the latest brand and the most recent year of the car for our test drive. After a few blocks of driving it, we both looked at each other and agreed that we were not finding the car suitable. The options were limited, and the features differed from what we expected. It felt like we were driving an older model. Once we returned to the salesperson, we made our complaint, and he told us that the car we drove was just the basic one. He then informed us that we could customize the vehicle to add the features that would satisfy our taste, and a new one would be built with all our unique specifications.

When you want to purchase a car, many manufacturers offer customization options that allow customers to personalize various aspects of the vehicle according to their preferences. "Building your car" allows buyers to create a vehicle that reflects their style, taste, and functional requirements. It also allows for a more personalized driving experience. It ensures that the car meets the specific needs and desires of the owner. Two people can have the same car brand, model, and year, yet the features may be different because they are customized according to what the buyer specified in their purchase request.

The Word of God also allows you to build your world. Everything you need to design the life you want is already contained in the Word of God. You can request that added feature if you do not have specific experiences. We know that the Word of God is the primary tool for creating the entire universe. And since you are also created in the image of God, the Word of God is your primary tool to co-create your world. If the Word of God framed the world, the Word of God can also frame your world.

Everything you need to design the life you want is already contained in the Word of God.

Many people accept living by default. Living by default means that you choose to accept all the limitations of your life. Some people feel they cannot escape their environmental conditions or genetic dispositions. But the truth is, you don't have to live by default. Get into the habit of rejecting every idea of living by default or accepting limitations imposed by circumstances. Instead, believe in the unseen realities and call them forth with the power of your words. *Like a new car, you can design your life by using God's Word and customize your world.*

> If the Word of God framed the world, the
> Word of God can also frame your world.

Faith is the substance of things hoped for and the evidence of things not seen. In other words, faith believes in unseen realities; to experience those realities, they must be called out by faith. Calling out unseen realities into the realm visible to the senses is how the faith of God operates. In Romans 4:17, the Bible says God gives life to the dead and *calls those things that do not exist as though they did.*

What do you call yourself? Do you describe yourself only in terms of what is visible today? You must see yourself beyond how you appear today and start calling yourself in the future state God has already designed for you. Search in the scriptures and find yourself in there. Find how God describes you in His Word, and then you can start calling yourself that.

In Genesis 15, God made a covenant with Abraham, promising him that he would have a son and that his descendants would be as numerous as the stars in the sky. However, Abraham and his wife Sarah were both advanced in age and had no children. Despite their natural limitations, they held onto the promise of God and trusted in His faithfulness.

In Genesis 17:5, God changed Abram's name to Abraham, which means "father of many nations," as a reminder of the covenant and the destiny God had planned for him. Likewise, Sarai's name was changed to Sarah, meaning "princess." These name changes symbolized their new identities as the parents of many descendants.

Although Abraham initially laughed at having a child in their old age, Sarah also struggled with doubt. However, in Hebrews 11:11 ESV, it is said that "By faith Sarah herself received power to conceive, even when she was past the age, since she considered him faithful who had promised."

Calling out unseen realities into the realm visible to the senses is how the faith of God operates.

Eventually, Sarah conceived and gave birth to a son named Isaac, fulfilling God's promise. *Through their faith and obedience, Abraham and Sarah spoke their reality into existence.* They believed in the impossible and trusted in God's Word, even when it seemed unlikely or impossible from a human standpoint.

Harnessing the Power of Your Words to Shape Your World: Four Essential Steps

Now that you understand the concept of speaking your reality into existence and customizing your world, the question arises: how do you effectively tap into the power of your words? How can you ensure that your words align with your desires and bring about the transformative changes you seek? Here are four (4) steps that can help you get started.

Align yourself with God's Word.

The foundation for speaking your reality into existence lies in aligning your words with the Word of God. The Word of God is powerful and has an inherent ability to bring about its fulfillment. Jeremiah 1:12 instructs us that God watches over His words to see them come true. Whenever you confess God's words, God makes Himself responsible for ensuring they come to pass. Also, Psalm 103:20 NKJV says, "Bless the Lord, you His angels, who excel in strength, who do His word, heeding the voice of His word." God's angels are always on guard and listening to enforce the Word of God.

When you declare God's words over your life in faith, it is as if God Himself is speaking them. Therefore, God watches over them to make sure what you say comes to pass, and His angels are listening to carry out every detail of the Word. The Scriptures contain promises, declarations, and principles that serve as a guide for shaping your world. Spend time studying and meditating on God's Word to gain a deeper understanding of His truth and the abundant life He desires for you.

Renew Your Mind.

The words we speak reflect the thoughts we harbor within. "A good man out of the good treasure of his heart brings forth good; and an evil man out of the evil treasure of his heart brings forth evil. For out of the abundance of the heart his mouth speaks." Luke 6: 45 NKJV. Your mouth will only speak what it can draw from what is in your heart. What you say is a reflection of what is in your heart. If you consistently describe yourself in a defeated or negative light, it is time to go inside and see what is in your heart. Because your mouth is a window to what is inside your heart, your words flow from what is in your heart. To shape your world with your words, renewing your mind and aligning your thoughts with God's perspective is essential. Fill your mind with positive, faith-filled thoughts by immersing yourself in uplifting books, teachings, and testimonies that reinforce God's promises and possibilities.

The Word of God is the agency by which faith is transmitted into your heart. "Consequently, faith comes from hearing the message, and the message is heard through the word about Christ." Romans 10: 17 NIV. The more you fill your heart by reading or hearing the Word of God, the more faith is generated.

Speak With Intention.

One thing I have observed from people who have cultivated a lifestyle of faith and have gotten results is that they are very intentional about their words. Be intentional about the words you speak. Avoid negative or limiting language that contradicts the reality you desire to create. Jesus said, "But I say to you that for every idle word men may speak, they will give account of it in the day of judgment. 3 For by your words you will be justified, and by your words you will be condemned."- Matthew 12: 36-37 NKJV. So, speak words of faith, affirmation, and gratitude. Declare the promises of God over your life and circumstances, believing that what you say will come to pass. Remember, your words have creative power, so choose them wisely.

Visualize Your Desired Reality.

Combine the power of words with the power of visualization. Let the Word of God create the images in your heart. Imagine and vividly picture the reality you desire to see manifest. As you speak words aligned with that vision, your faith will grow stronger, reinforcing your belief in the manifestation of your desire.

Remember, shaping your world with your words is an ongoing process that requires consistency, faith, and patience. It may take time for the seeds you sow through your spoken words to bear fruit, but remain steadfast in your belief and continue speaking in alignment with God's promises. By aligning your words with God's Word, renewing your mind, speaking with intention, and visualizing your desired reality, you will gradually experience the transformative power of your words in shaping the world around you.

Framework For Effective Confession of the Word of God

> "Let your conduct be without covetousness; be content with such things as you have. For He Himself has said, "I will never leave you nor forsake you." So we may boldly say: "The LORD is my helper; I will not fear. What can man do to me?"
>
> **Hebrews 25:12 NKJV**

The above Bible verses provide an effective framework for confessing the Word of God. This framework is contained in these two phrases, "For He Himself has said;" "So we may boldly say." What gives us boldness to declare the Words of God is because He Himself has said. Because He has said it, therefore we may boldly declare it. Search the scriptures diligently for what God has spoken concerning you and your situation, and then begin to boldly declare them.

Prayers:

1. Ask God for wisdom to choose words that align with His purposes and ask for discernment to recognize the impact of your words.

2. Pray for grace to speak positive words over your life and situations, aligning them with God's purposes.

3. Pray for awareness of the influence your words have on others and ask for grace to inspire and uplift them with your words.

4. Pray that God gives you the strength to break any negative speech patterns and replace them with words of life and hope.

5. Ask for God's protection from the impact of harmful words, both spoken by others and unintentionally spoken by yourself.

Confession:

The words I speak are powerful. I choose my words carefully, knowing that they shape the realities of my life. I will speak words of life to every situation that I face. I will boldly declare the Words of God out of my mouth because His Words spoken in faith are a creative force.

Reflective Questions

1. How does the concept of framing your world with words resonate with your personal beliefs and experiences?

2. Reflect on instances in your life when words, wheth-

er spoken by you or someone else, had a profound impact on your circumstances or outlook. What did you learn from those experiences?

3. Consider the power of spoken words in shaping your relationships, career, and personal development. Are there specific examples of how your words have influenced these areas?

4. In what ways have you harnessed the "spirit of faith" to speak positive, transformative words into your life and the lives of others?

5. Think about your current life situation. How would you like to see your world framed differently, and how can you begin using your words to bring about that change?

6. Have there been instances when you felt limited or confined by negative self-talk or external influences? How can the concept of framing your world with words help you break free from such limitations?

Action Note

Please use this section to write down things you will start doing based on what you have learned in this chapter.

CHAPTER 7

Obtain Your Good Report

There was a time in my life when I was deeply captivated by the idea of winning a Nobel Peace Prize. This esteemed award is bestowed upon individuals or organizations who have made significant contributions to promoting global peace and resolving conflicts. My intense fascination with this prize can be traced back to my upbringing in the Northern region of Nigeria, where I witnessed numerous interethnic and religious conflicts that plagued the area. My experiences influenced my passion to be a peace practitioner. Even while my desire and passion to become a peace practitioner were in the early stages, I had my eyes on the coveted Nobel Peace Prize.

The Nobel Peace Prize is a distinct category within the Nobel Prize system, and these prizes are among the most prestigious accolades in the world. They honor outstanding achievements in various fields, including Physics, Chemistry, Medicine or Physiology, Literature, Peace, and Economic Sciences. Winning a Nobel Prize is widely regarded as one of the highest honors, both in the realms of academia and peace advocacy.

Like the Nobel Prizes, specific awards emerge as the ultimate forms of recognition and accomplishment in different domains and based on individual aspirations. Winning a Nobel Prize can be likened to achieving an Olympic medal, symbolizing the pinnacle of success in sports. Olympic athletes dedicate years to rigorous training to compete at the highest levels, aiming to stand proudly atop the podium. Similarly, in entertainment, securing Grammy Awards for musical excellence or Academy Awards (Oscars) for cinematic achievements represents the highest recognition for talent and excellence in their respective fields. You can think of many more awards that recognize individual excellence testifying to the recipients' reputational achievements.

****

> "Through their faith, the people in days of old earned a good reputation."
>
> **Hebrews 11:2 NLT**

In this book, we have considered notable examples of what can be accomplished through the act of faith in God. The examples are from Hebrews chapter 11, also known as the "Faith Hall of Fame" or Faith Chapter because of the various figures from the Old Testament who demonstrated great faith. The verse from this chapter quoted above means that these elders or figures from the past mentioned in the preceding verses were highly regarded or received a commendable reputation because of their faith. In the context of the overall chapter, the author emphasizes the importance of faith as the foundation of a righteous and pleasing relationship with God. The individuals mentioned in the chapter are celebrated for their unwavering trust and belief in God, which led them to act in ways that were pleasing to Him and positively impacted others. Their faith in God was a critical factor in their righteous and praiseworthy lives, and their actions and choices were well-regarded because they trusted in God.

Like the Nobel Peace Prize, Olympic medal, and other notable achievements that give individuals high standing in various fields, faith earned the elders an excellent reputation and made them stand above the crowd.

It's Your Turn

The stories and great feats of faith don't end with the elders mentioned in the "Faith Hall of Fame." You also have been given the opportunity to obtain a good testimony with God and cement your name in the "Faith Hall of Fame" through your acts of faith.

Hebrews 12:1 NKJV says, "Therefore we also, since we are surrounded by so great a cloud of witnesses, let us lay aside every weight, and the sin which so easily ensnares us, and let us run with endurance the race that is set before us."

From these stories of faith, you have been adequately equipped with examples to guide your faith journey. These examples serve as frameworks and patterns of what is possible and what can be achieved through faith, and their purpose is to encourage you whenever you step out in faith. And now, I am challenging you to run the race set before you. Your race and the challenges you will face may be different from those that we have discussed or those described in the Bible, yet the same principles of faith are consistently applied in all cases.

To conclude this book, I will be sharing with you four (4) principles of faith that you can follow as you consider your next move of faith.

Know the Will of God

F. F. Bosworth once said, "Faith begins where the will of God is known." If you don't know God's will, you can't have faith. This is because you cannot boldly claim by faith a blessing that you are not sure God is offering. That is why the Bible says, "Therefore do not be unwise, but understand what the will of the Lord is." (Ephesians 5:17 NKJV) To exercise faith, there is no room for vagueness where you are unsure if it is the will of God to do something for you. You must be absolutely convinced that God can do it and is willing to demonstrate His power on that issue for you. If one thing is sure to weaken your faith, it is the uncertainty that God is willing to do for you what you are hoping for. Nothing weakens your faith more than an uncertainty of God's will.

In Matthew chapter 8, a leper came to Jesus and said to Him, "Lord, if You are willing, you can make me clean." Now, this leper knew that Jesus had the power or the ability to make him clean. But he needed clarification on whether it was in His will to do so. Oh, how often do we forfeit the promises and blessings of God simply because we are not sure if He is willing. In this passage, Jesus settled this question of His willingness for all time and eternity with this declarative statement, "I am willing; be cleansed." The Bible records that immediately, his leprosy was cleansed. Once this man laid hold of the will of God, his healing became automatic because he could then have faith for it.

You may be wondering, how then can I know for sure the will of God for my situation?

The simple answer is the will of God is only revealed

in His Words. So, to know for sure what the will of God is, you must look into His Words and what He has promised as His will. Once you get acquainted with the Word of God, you come to fully grasp His will, and that is how you can exercise genuine faith. Romans 10:17 says faith comes by hearing the Word of God. The measure of your faith will be directly proportional to the revelation knowledge of God that you have through His Word. It is through hearing that you come to know what the will of God is, and that is what brings about faith. Understand the will of God for your life through His promises.

Get acquainted with the Word of God so thoroughly that the conscious application of faith becomes an automatic, unconscious action of faith. The Word of God and His promises should be so natural to you that when you apply them, it is not by conscious effort but by unconscious acts that are prompted by the deposited faith in your heart.

Be Convinced of The Promises of God for You

Once you know the will of God, the next thing is to be absolutely convinced of those promises for your life. I have observed that many people believe in the Word and promises of God, but not for themselves. They believe the Word of God is true and can happen for anyone, but they are not convinced it can happen for them. Believing in

God's promises alone is not sufficient. You must be confident about the promises for yourself and that what God promised can happen for you.

In chapter 3 of this book, we discussed how you can build your persuasion or conviction in the Word of God. I will encourage you to read again the steps that can help you to be absolutely convinced of the promises of God. One important thing that I want to stress here is the need to meditate on the Word of God constantly. God told Joshua, "This Book of the Law shall not depart from your mouth, but you shall meditate in it day and night, that you may observe to do according to all that is written in it. For then, you will make your way prosperous, and then you will have good success." Joshua 1:8 NKJV. Meditating on the Word of God increases our capacity to receive it into our lives. Meditation is the vehicle by which you can transmit the Word of God into your spirit, where faith can emanate. Cultivate the habit of constantly meditating on the promises of God.

Declare Authoritatively the Promises of God Over Your Life

The primary way to release your faith is through your mouth. Faith is of the heart but can only be released with the mouth. We pray for things not already provided, but we confess and accept the ones already provided. Once you become convinced of the will of God revealed through His Words, all you can do is accept it and begin to confess and declare it authoritatively because it has already been provided for. If I tell you that I have already paid for your car, do you still pray to me to give you a car, or do you go to the dealer and declare that someone has already paid for it and you are there to pick it up? It is the same with the Word of God; *it is yours to take once it is provided.*

Take Corresponding Actions

Faith is doing what God tells you to do, then expecting God will do what He tells you He would do. The proof of your faith is the actions you take in response to the Word of God. The Bible clearly states, "Faith without works is dead." If you claim to have faith, you must show it by the necessary active steps. Without these corresponding actions, your faith is dead. What makes your faith come alive after you know and are convinced of the will of God, is that you release your faith through speaking. You must follow up by taking necessary actions to support your beliefs. Let us go back to the example of paying for your car. Once I make my intentions known to you, you are convinced I have paid for your car. You have taken it further by constantly confessing that you have received a car from me, but you have never gone to the dealership to claim it. How ridiculous would it be if all you do is sit and confess what you have but never take the action required to possess it? It is the same with faith. Your actions must correspond with what you believe and what you are speaking.

Prayer:

1. Pray that in all you do, God will give you a perfect revelation of His will.

2. Ask God for enablement and strength to take the necessary corresponding actions of faith.

3. Pray that your life will reflect positive results of faith and that you will not be ashamed in your faith walk.

Confession:

Father, thank You for the knowledge of Your will that is made abundantly clear to me. Thank You because it is given to me to know the mysteries of the kingdom of heaven. As I declare the Words of God that are revealed to me in faith, and take actions on them, the Holy Spirit works in me to confirm the Words of God in my life. As a child of God, I speak the words of God with authority and power.

Reflective Questions

1. What does a "good report" mean to you personally? How will you define and measure success in your own journey of faith?

2. How has the journey through this book reshaped your understanding of faith and the significance of obtaining a good report?

3. Reflect on your own life and the moments when you've witnessed the impact of faith. In what ways has faith played a role in your accomplishments and overcoming challenges?

4. Think about the elders mentioned in Hebrews 11 who obtained a good report through faith. How do their stories inspire you to pursue your own remarkable journey of faith?

5. What specific actions or decisions can you take today to step out in faith and work towards obtaining your own good report in life?

Action Note

Please use this section to write down things you will start doing based on what you have learned in this chapter.

ACKNOWLEDGEMENT

Above all, I express my deepest gratitude to God Almighty for the inspiration to embark on this writing journey. Without His divine guidance, this book would not have come to fruition.

I am indebted to a group of remarkable individuals who played pivotal roles in bringing this work to life. Kofoworola Ayodeji and Charlidza Pierre, thank you for your invaluable contributions in reading the first draft and providing insightful edits. Your perspectives enriched the narrative in ways I could not have achieved alone.

Special thanks to Bishop Paul Aigboje for his kindness, generosity, and the privilege to serve in his ministry.

To Reverend and Pastor Malomo, your ceaseless prayers and unwavering support have been a source of strength throughout this endeavor. Your spiritual guidance has been a cornerstone in the success of this book.

A special appreciation goes to my parents Mr. Ola Adeniji and Mrs. Grace Oyeneye for their boundless love and encouragement. Their belief in my abilities has been a constant motivation, and I am truly grateful for their unwavering support. To my siblings, Olasunkanmi Oyeneye, Funmilayo Bello, and Tosin Olojede, I am immensely grateful for all your love and belief in me.

Last but certainly not least, I extend my deepest appreciation to my wife, Adijat Oyeneye. Her steadfast presence by my side, offering unyielding support and encouragement, has been my rock. She was the first to read the manuscript, providing constructive feedback that significantly enhanced the quality of this work. Her insights and willingness to engage with my ideas have been instrumental in shaping the narrative.

This book is a testament to the collaborative efforts of these exceptional individuals, and I am profoundly thankful for the role each of you has played in making this dream a reality.

STAY CONNECTED

youtube.com/@ThoughtsOnTheseThings

https://www.tiktok.com/@thoughtsonthesethings

https://www.instagram.com/thoughtsonthesethings/

facebook/thoughtsonthesethings

If you wish to post about this book on your social media, please use any of my social media tags.

Milton Keynes UK
Ingram Content Group UK Ltd.
UKHW050943260624
444769UK00013B/518